CW01640902

Welcome to iPad The Complete Manual

The iPad has taken the world by storm, integrating itself into every environment you can think of. In the classroom, office and home, the device offers endless opportunities for improving how we learn, work and play. Today the likes of the new 9.7-inch iPad Pro and iPad mini 4 show us a type of power, versatility and portability we could only imagine several years ago. This edition of iPad The Complete Manual shows you how to harness that power to enhance your lifestyle and productivity. Read on to familiarise yourself with your gadget, navigate the set up process and master the basics of Apple's fantastic built-in apps, from Apple Music to News, and third-party apps like Paper by 53.

iPad
The Complete Manual

Imagine Publishing Ltd
Richmond House
33 Richmond Hill
Bournemouth
Dorset BH2 6EZ
☎ +44 (0) 1202 586200
Website: www.imagine-publishing.co.uk
Twitter: @Books_Imagine
Facebook: www.facebook.com/ImagineBookazines

Publishing Director
Aaron Asadi

Head of Design
Ross Andrews

Editor In Chief
Jon White

Production Editor
Sanne de Boer

Senior Art Editor
Greg Whitaker

Assistant Designer
Sophie Ward

Photographer
James Sheppard

Printed by
William Gibbons, 26 Planetary Road, Willenhall, West Midlands, WV13 3XT

Distributed in the UK, Eire & the Rest of the World by
Marketforce, 5 Churchill Place, Canary Wharf, London, E14 5HU
Tel 0203 787 9060 www.marketforce.co.uk

Distributed in Australia by
Gordon & Gotch Australia Pty Ltd, 26 Rodborough Road, Frenchs Forest, NSW, 2086 Australia
Tel +61 2 9972 8800 www.gordongotch.com.au

ISBN 9781785463099

Part of the iCreate bookazine series

IMAGINE PUBLISHING

Contents

What you can find inside the bookazine

Introducing iPad

The apps

Access millions of songs straight from your iPad thanks to Apple Music. Read up on page 52

Easily become an iPad expert

Introducing the iPad

What makes the iPad one of the best tablets available? It's time to find out...

The original iPad completely transformed the tablet market. Its beautiful screen, portability and fantastic built-in apps struck a chord with consumers and critics alike. Apple added to its tablet repertoire in 2012 when it launched the iPad mini – giving users a new choice that centred on even greater portability and an attractive price point. Most recently, Apple released two new additions to the iPad family: the iPad mini 4 and the formidable iPad Pro – the biggest, most powerful iPad ever!

Considering the long battery life and exceptional build quality, the iPad is a tablet built for anyone who wants to work and play anywhere. On top of all this, the release of iOS 9 and the subsequent updates have brought many exciting new features, so there really hasn't been a better time to join the iPad revolution.

Fig 1 The simple, user-friendly Calendar app interface actually works well for complex agenda management

Fig 2 The Clock app can deal with alarms, world times and you can use it as a stopwatch if necessary

Get organised

The iPad is packed full of useful functionality straight out of the box, and the tools to get yourself organised are all included. First up is the Calendar app, which looks quite basic at first glance, but when you dig below the surface you start to realise that the simplistic interface is actually very useful when handling complex calendars (Fig 1). You can deal with more than one calendar at once and accept invitations automatically.

The Reminders app lets you quickly add tasks that need to be completed at certain times and schedule alerts to remind you. You can even set Reminders to activate when you reach a particular location. The Clock app will wake you up with an alarm every day, and also includes timers that can be used for time-dependent tasks (Fig 2). We shouldn't forget the Contacts app which will help you store details for every person you might need to contact.

Get work done

The iPad is not just designed for home use, it can be utilised for use at work too. The Mail app allows you to preview Office documents when they are received and you can also use the extra screen size

and well thought-out keyboard for writing things down using the Notes app. You can also utilise the Maps app to help you get to meetings and plan ahead so that you know how much travelling time you can expect and what public transport will get you there.

As time has passed, the potential of the iPad in the workplace has been realised and there are thousands of apps available to let you undertake specific tasks. However, for the basics and day-to-day work tasks that take up most of your time, the iPad is able, from a software and hardware perspective, to help you get everything done that you need to.

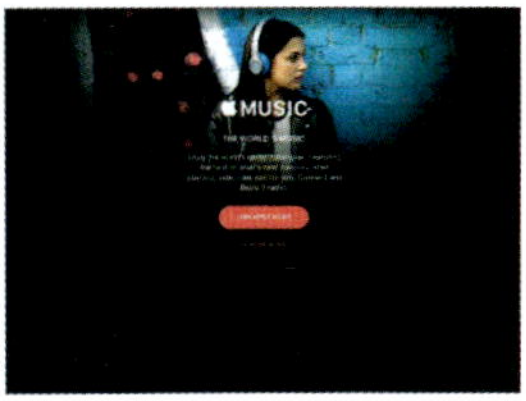

Fig 3 The Music app is now geared towards the Apple Music streaming service whereby you can listen to anything at any time

Enjoy yourself

The iPad is perfect for keeping yourself and your family entertained anywhere. The Videos app lets you watch movies for hours at a time before a charge is needed, perfect for long distance flights, and the sound quality is superb through headphones and even the external speaker. The Music app is also on hand to play all of your synced tunes and the introduction of the Apple Music streaming service means you can listen to whatever you want, when you want (Fig 3). The inclusion of iTunes (Fig 4) takes your entertainment

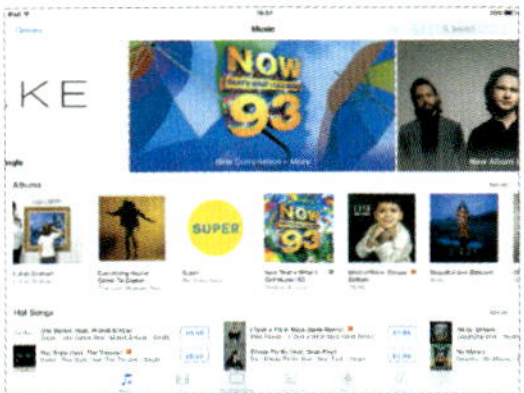

Fig 4 Music, films, audiobooks and TV shows are all available to buy through the vast catalogue in the iTunes app

How the iPad can improve your life

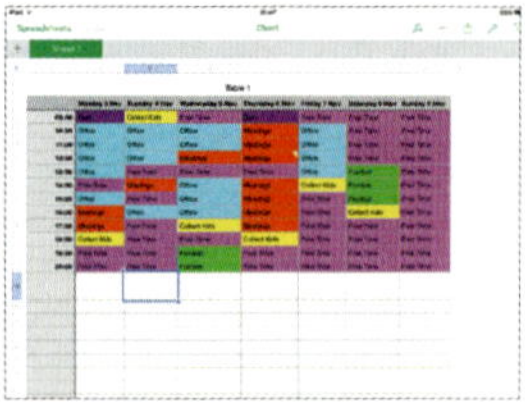

Productivity

The iWork suite of apps lets you produce spreadsheets, presentations and documents easily, while the touch interface makes work fun.

Lifestyle

Whether you want to make and record beautiful music or create home videos, you can do it all in style on an iPad using the iLife suite of apps.

Entertainment

The native iBooks reader lets you purchase and read eBooks that look like paper titles. You can also watch full-screen videos and play music whenever you want to.

An introduction to iPad

> There are many situations where the iPad is perfect for providing entertainment

options to a whole new level. From music to movies and from TV shows to iBooks, everything you need is available to purchase and download straight to the iPad. You can also create your own keepsakes using the camera or by transferring a photo collection to the iPad for viewing whenever you want to remember a good time. There are many situations where the iPad is perfect for providing entertainment for the whole family.

The iPad Pro

With the release of iOS 9, Apple also gave the world the much larger iPad Pro. Lighter than a MacBook, but bigger than your traditional iPad, the Pro allows its user even more creativity. Its screen, while

iPad accessories

Case
iPads don't like being dropped, so a sturdy case will help you ensure that your investment lasts. Cases like the QDOS Libris also add extra functionality that is extremely useful

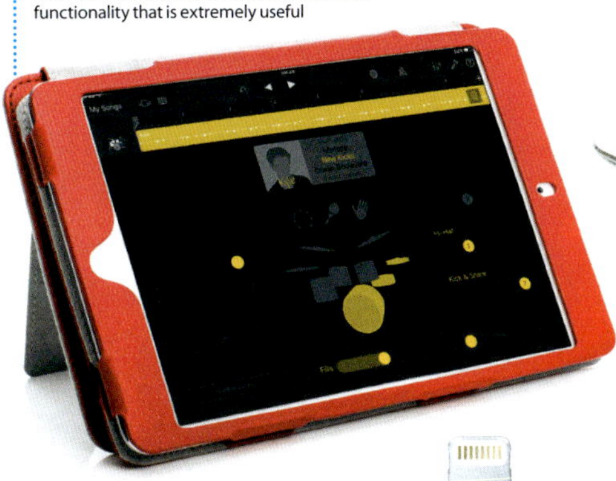

Cover
There are many thin covers available that clip to the back of your iPad and cover the screen, providing protection without adding bulk to your device

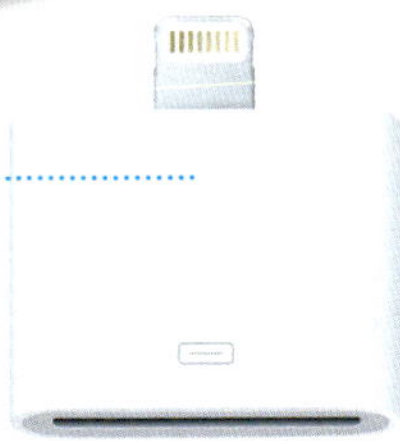

Lightning to 30-pin Adaptor
This adaptor will let you connect a huge range of accessories that were designed for previous generation iPads to the latest versions, which will open up the number of accessories you can use

Fling analogue joystick
If you love gaming on your iPad but miss the traditional controls of consoles, this analogue joystick controller for iPad is for you

Apple Pencil
If you're hoping to get the newest addition to the iPad family, the iPad Pro, you can't miss out on the Apple Pencil. More than a stylus, this self-powered and highly responsive gadget lets you interact with your iPad like never before

Headphones
iPads are capable of providing very good quality sound, but the addition of a high-end set of headphones, like these Sennheisers, will improve the sound quality even more

An introduction to iPad

Fig 5 The iOS 9 News app takes content from your favourite news sources and delivers it in one handy digest

obviously physically large, is also home to 5.6 million pixels, giving it the highest resolution display of any iOS device. You can edit 4K video, and see the quality oozing from the screen. Its bigger screen also allows for the native apps to work more spectacularly. The bigger space gives more room for features, including a whole extra run of keyboard in GarageBand. Its new four-speak audio system also means it is perfect for playing films at super high quality, making it much easier to get lost in a new world.

Apple have introduced the Apple Pencil as an accompaniment for the iPad Pro, making sketching out your creative ideas much easier than simply using your finger.

Top iPad applications

BBC iPlayer
Catch up and enjoy some of the finest televisual treats around with this sleek viewing portal.

Netflix
Log in to your account and stream a varied collection of films and TV shows straight to your iPad.

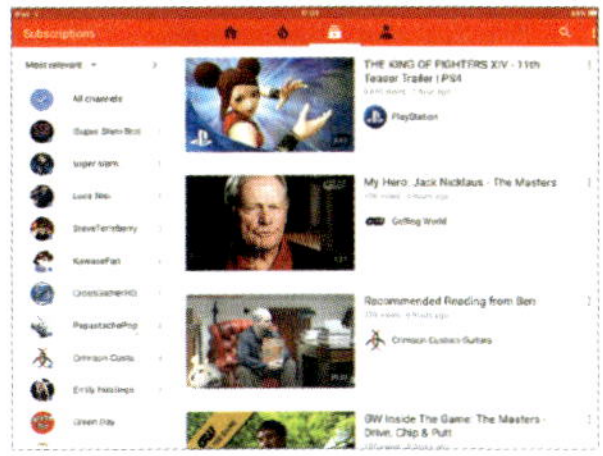

YouTube
If you're short of visual entertainment on your iPad, this free download is packed full of essential viewing.

TuneIn Radio
Find the music that matters to you by streaming it from thousands of digital stations from all around the world.

Amazon
This easy-to-use app lets you search for items to buy quickly and easily thanks to a simple interface.

Evernote
With its intuitive interface, you can take notes, annotate images and access them from anywhere.

Brushes 3
With a wide range of brushes, effects and layers, this app lets you draw and paint freely using your finger.

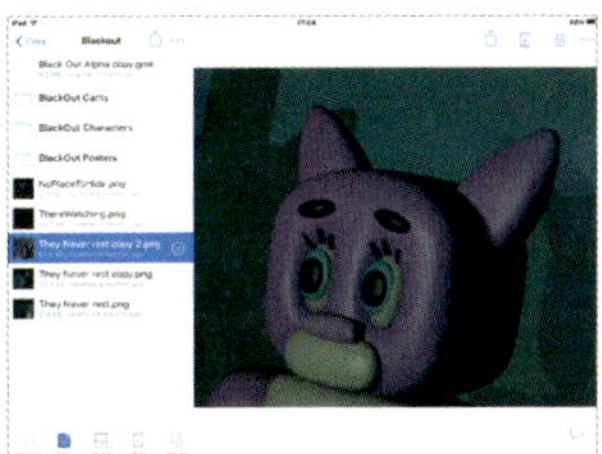

Dropbox
Ensure that you always have your most important files close to hand thanks to this essential cloud storage app.

Amplitube for iPad
Plug in your guitar via the iRig adaptor and strum freely through a wide range of amps and effect pedals.

New iOS 9 multitasking enhancements mean you can now keep two apps open on the same screen with Split View

Set up your device

We show you how to activate your iPad for the first time and familiarise yourself with what it has to offer. Here we're using an iPad Air, but the process is the same for setting up an iPad mini or Pro

If your device is new or has been recently reset you should be greeted with the Apple logo

Set up your device

1 Turn your iPad on To turn on your iPad for the first time, press and hold the On/Off button (the lozenge-shaped button on the top right of the tablet) for about three seconds. If your iPad is new or has been recently reset you should be greeted with the Apple logo and then, after ten seconds or so (the time may vary depending on your model), a plain screen with 'Hello' written on it (Fig 1).

2 Resetting a pre-owned iPad If, when you turn your iPad on via the On/Off button, you are taken straight to the Home Screen, then your iPad is already activated. If you wish to reset the iPad so you can set it up as new, go to the Settings app and scroll down to the Reset option and Erase All Contents And Settings. You can then follow this tutorial to activate your iPad as new.

3 Slide to unlock At the plain-looking iPad screen (as shown in Fig 1), you need to slide your finger to the right across the arrow at the bottom of the screen to continue. At this screen the iPad is locked. You will need to perform the sliding motion every time you wish to wake the iPad up, but every time you're required to do this, the screen will tell you that you need to swipe, and in which direction.

4 Waking up the iPad If at any point during the activation process the iPad goes to 'sleep' (the screen goes blank), usually because it was left unattended, you can wake it up simply by pressing the Home button (the circular one at the bottom-centre of the iPad's front) or tapping the On/Off button (don't hold it). You'll then have to unlock your iPad.

5 Select your language Once you've unlocked your iPad, you will see a short list of common languages to choose from. If the language that you'd like is not in this list, tap the downwards arrow. You will then be presented with a long list of different languages. The language you choose here will be the language that your device is set to. Tap the blue and white arrow in the top-right corner.

6 Select your Country or Region Now, similar to choosing your language, you will have a short list of countries/regions to choose from (Fig 2). If your country or region is not in the list, tap 'Show More…' and pick yours from there. This will determine the apps that are available in the App Store and the various media available from the iTunes app, as well as the correct currency.

If you have a newer iDevice, you can set up Touch ID in this process to unlock your device faster

Fig 1, Turn on Fire up your brand new iPad

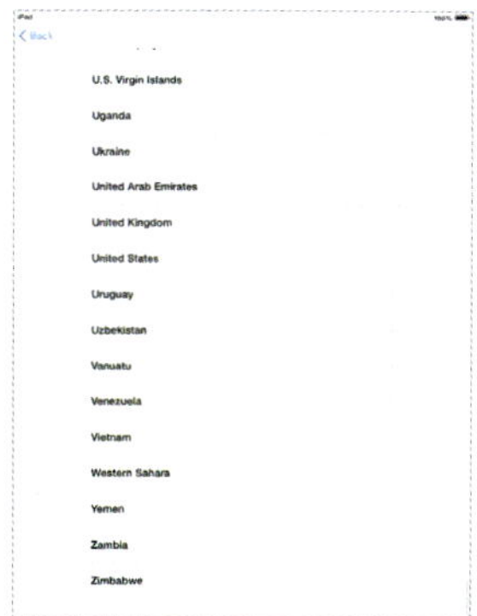

Fig 2, Select your region This affects apps

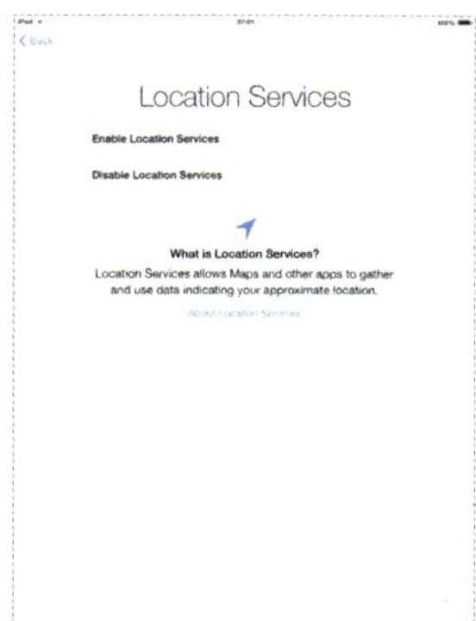

Fig 3, Location Services This is used by apps

Set up your device

7 Location Services The next part of the process is dedicated to your device's Location Services (Fig 3). This allows apps to gather and use data indicating your approximate location, which is incredibly useful if you ever lose your device. For a more detailed explanation on the service, tap 'What is Location Services?' towards the bottom of the screen. Tap 'Done' when you've finished.

8 Enable or Disable You must either enable or disable the Location Services service by tapping on your chosen option – there is no option to skip the step. If you are still unsure of the purpose of this feature and need more information then don't worry; you can activate it later from the Settings app in the Home screen. Tap 'Next' to continue the activation process.

9 Connect to a Wi-Fi network Your iPad will be able to connect to the internet wirelessly via a Wi-Fi connection. If you have a Wi-Fi network set up in your house it will appear in the menu (Fig 4). Tap on it and you will need to enter your password using the on-screen keyboard. When you've entered the password, tap the Join button either on the keyboard or the dialog box.

10 If you don't have a Wi-Fi connection... If you can't access a Wi-Fi connection, but you do have a computer with iTunes installed, you can continue the activation by connecting your iPad to the computer via the supplied USB cable and then choosing the 'Connect to iTunes' option beneath any other wireless networks the iPad could pick up.

11 Set Up iPad The next screen you'll see will present you with three options: Set Up as New iPad, Restore from iCloud Backup, and Restore from iTunes Backup (Fig 5). You will most likely want to choose the first option, which requires no more than a tap of the 'Next' button in the top right to continue with the activation (Step 14). However, we will also look at the other choices...

12 Restore from iCloud Backup You should choose this option if you have an iCloud account that has a backup attached to it. Once you've chosen and tapped 'Next' you'll have to enter the Apple ID of the account that has the backup, and its password. You'll then be able to restore the iPad from the backup. New iPad owners won't use this.

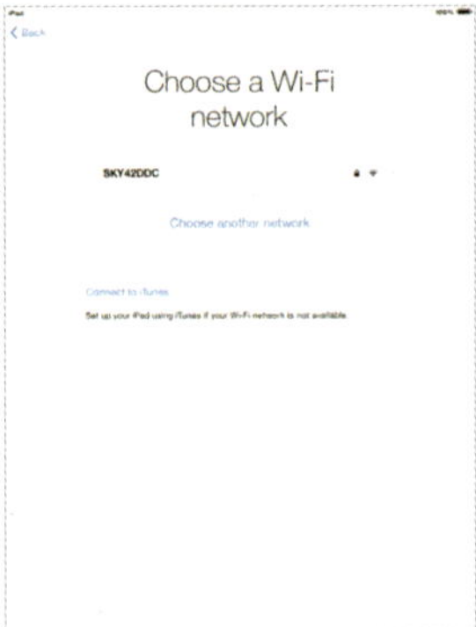

Fig 4, Connect to Wi-Fi Scan for networks

Fig 5, Set Up iPad Choose an option

Fig 6, Apple ID You need one of these

You can also activate your device via iTunes by connecting it to a computer via USB

13 Restore from iTunes Backup If you choose this option you'll be able to restore your iPad from a backup kept on your desktop computer in iTunes. Connect your iPad to your computer via the USB cable and select the backup you want to use from iTunes. Note that you can also set the iPad as a new one (as if you tapped the 'Set Up as New iPad' button in Step 11) from here.

14 Apple ID The Apple ID, which you create in the next step of the activation, is one of the most important things you will do during the process (Fig 6). A tap of the 'What is an Apple ID?' link at the bottom of the screen tells you why ownership of an Apple ID is essential. You will need one to download apps from the App Store, buy songs from iTunes and purchase books from iBooks.

15 Create an Apple ID If you have yet to create an Apple ID, it's incredibly simple to do so, and you do can do it from the comfort of your iPad. Tap the Create A Free Apple ID button and you'll have to enter your birthday (which will be used in case you forget your password), your name, and the email address that will eventually become your Apple ID.

16 Sign In with an Apple ID Due to the exceptional success of Apple programs like iTunes, you may already have an Apple ID without so much as touching an iPad, Mac, iPhone, or iPod. If you have one, tap Sign In with an Apple ID and enter your ID and password. If you know you own one but can't remember the details, tap 'Forgot Apple ID or Password?' and you'll be able to retrieve it.

17 Read the Terms & Conditions After signing in with either your brand new or existing Apple ID, you will be presented with a screen of Terms and Conditions (Fig 7) that relate to your iPad and the services that you will be using, such as iCloud, Game Center and so on. If you wish to read them on a larger screen, you can email them to yourself by tapping the 'Send by Email' button.

18 All about iCloud After 30 seconds or so, you will have the opportunity to set up one of the most revolutionary services Apple has created: iCloud – a fantastic cloud service that enables you to wirelessly keep your contacts, emails and calendars across multiple devices without you having to do anything. Tap 'What is iCloud' (Fig 8) to find out more about how it can benefit your life.

An Apple ID enables you to buy music, movies and books straight from the comfort of your device

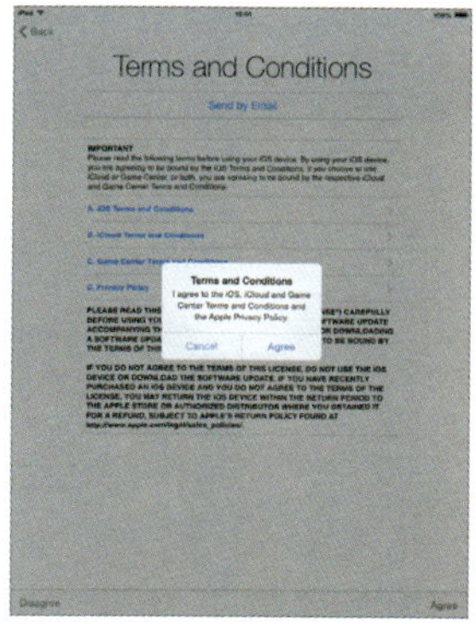

Fig 7, T&Cs You must agree to these

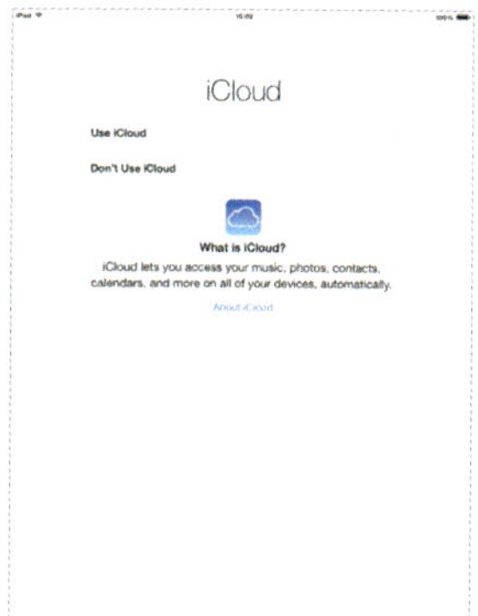

Fig 8, iCloud There to make your life easier

Fig 9, Find My iPad Handy to have on

Set up your device

Fig 10, Diagnostics Tracks your data

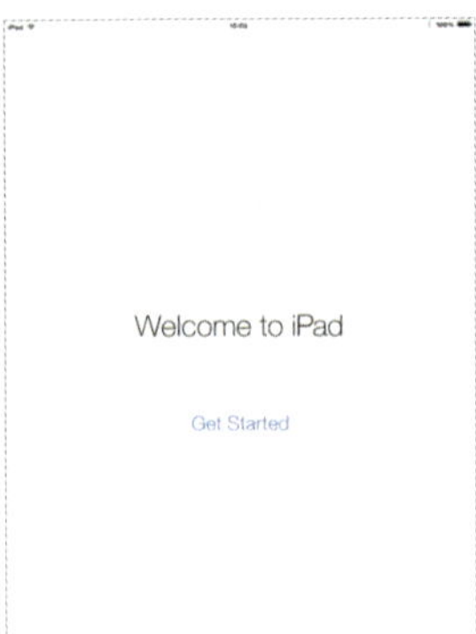

Fig 11, Set up complete! Start using your iPad

Fig 12, Start using your iPad Have fun!

19 **Enable or disable iCloud** Tap the top option to enable iCloud – it's free (although there is the option to pay to increase your storage space, which you can do in Settings). If you choose not to enable it, you will miss the opportunity to set up Find My iPad in the next step of the process. You can, however, enable it from the Settings app once you've completed the activation.

20 **The Find My iPad service** If you misplace your iPad then Find My iPad will help you locate it on a map, play a sound or display a message. You can activate this service to sync the location of your device with your iCloud (Fig 9). If you lose your iPad then you can access the service from an iPhone, iPod touch or computer by visiting **www.icloud.com**.

21 **Diagnostics and Usage** The next screen deals with diagnostics and usage data (Fig 10). Basically, Apple likes to keep track of how its products are performing, so this screen allows you to send diagnostic data straight to Apple. If you wish to keep your information private, opt for 'Don't Send'. You can change your answer after activation from the Settings app, in the 'About' tab.

22 **Your last chance to restart** The diagnostics screen offers you once last chance to restart the activation process if you're not happy with the choices you've made. To restart the process, tap the Home button (the circular button at the bottom of the iPad) once, and a menu should pop up. You will then find the option to restart the activation, where you can make the choices you want.

23 **Set up is complete!** Congratulations! You have now worked your way through the entire set-up process. A screen will confirm that the process is complete (Fig 11), so what are you waiting for? Tap on the 'Get Started' button to start using your iPad! If you press the Home button now to restart the procedure, you will just be taken to the Home Screen instead.

24 **Start using your iPad** You'll be presented with your Home Screen (Fig 12), so start tapping on icons to launch apps and find your way around and experiment with the gestures needed to operate your new device. Tap the Settings app and you'll have access to countless options, including ones that can reset the choices you made during the activation process.

You can change most of the choices you made during activation in the Settings app

The iOS 9 Home screen

Wi-Fi
This icon shows that you're connected to a network. See the icons below for more info

Time
You can change the format of the device's clock in the Settings app

Battery
This little icon will tell you how much battery power you have left

The apps
The heart and soul of ios 9. Tap on an icon to launch the app

The Dock
Many people choose to place their most used apps here in the Dock

Wallpaper
Your background is called the wallpaper. You can change it from the Settings app

Common icons

Wi-Fi
This icon shows that your device is successfully connected to the internet via a Wi-Fi network

Lock
This tells you that your device is locked. Slide your finger across the bottom of the screen to unlock it

Screen orientation lock
If you've set your device to stop switching from landscape to portrait, then you'll see this icon

3G
If you see this icon then you're connected to the web over a 3G network. Not all iPads have this

Do Not Disturb
If your device is set to Do Not Disturb mode then this icon will appear in the top-middle of the screen

Alarm
Set an Alarm in the Clock app and this icon will appear in the top right, telling you that your Alarm is active

4G
If you have a newer device, you may have access to the internet over 4G; in which case, this icon will be displayed

Battery
The icon in the top-right shows you how much power you have left. A lightning bolt will show it's charging

Location Services
The Location Services icon will appear to tell you that your device is determining your current location

Airplane mode
If you put your device in Airplane mode then you can't access the internet or Bluetooth. Look for this icon

Activity
The Activity icon will show up when something is happening on your device. Continue using it as normal

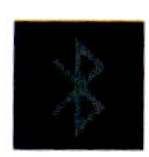

Bluetooth
If you're paired with another device via Bluetooth, then this icon will show in the top-right-corner of the screen

How to use your iPad

Learn how you can navigate and control your tablet with just a few button presses

Using an iPad is all about touch. There are very few hardware buttons included aside from the Home button on the front, the On/Off button at the top and the volume and mute keys on the side – so it's amazing that the iPad is capable of doing so much. As well as the basic tasks that you would expect it to do – turn on and off, go on standby, etc – you can use its incredible multi-touch screen in combination with the buttons to multitask and arrange and manage your apps to your heart's content. Here are some of the basic actions you need to know about when navigating your iPad.

Turn your iPad on and off

1 The power button Hold down the On/Off button (at the top of the iPad) for a couple of seconds to turn the iPad on from a cold start. The 'Slide to Unlock' screen will appear quite quickly.

2 Turn off Hold the On/Off button for a few seconds when the iPad is on.

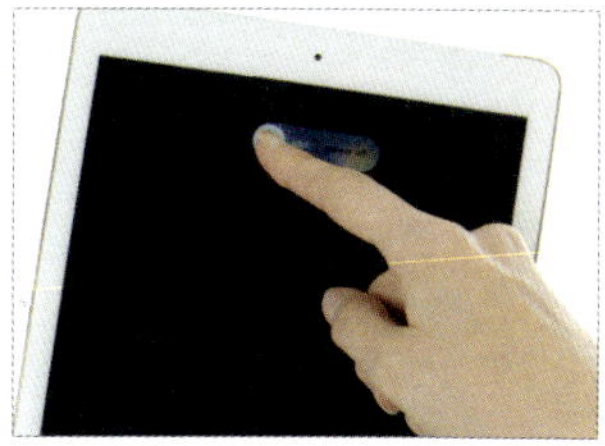

3 Slide to turn off Slide the slider at the top to turn your iPad off.

Put your iPad to sleep

1 Don't hold it Press the On/Off button as normal, but do not hold it down for too long.

2 Standby mode The screen will go blank and the iPad is now in standby mode ready to start again.

Charge your iPad

1 Use the kit Plug the charger cable into the bottom of the iPad.

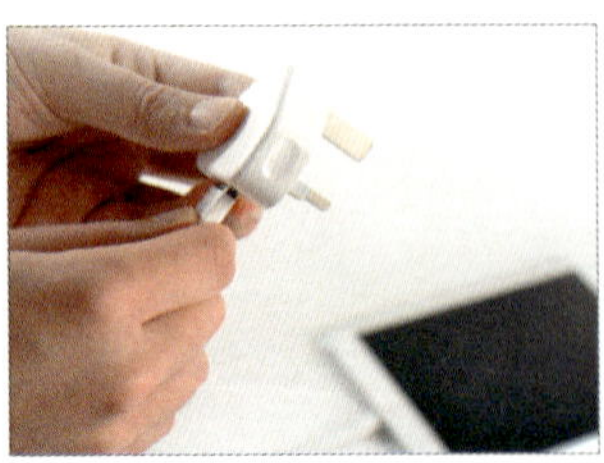

2 Plug it Plug the cable into the AC adaptor that comes with the iPad.

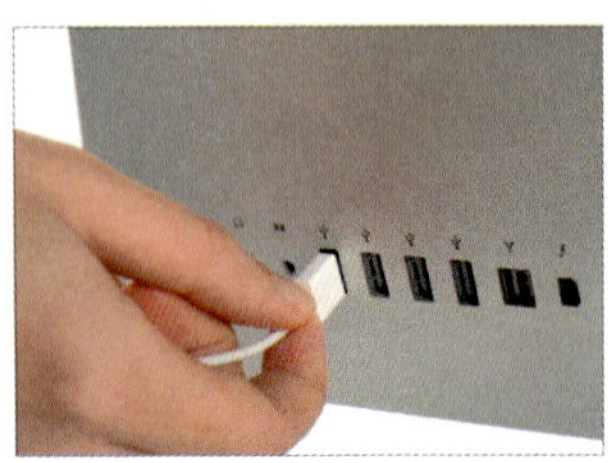

3 USB You can also charge the iPad by USB, but it's not the quickest way.

Multitasking

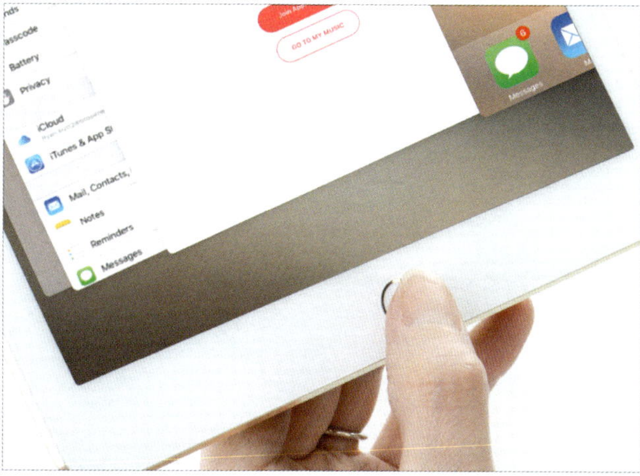

1 Double-tap Home No matter what app you are in or where you are, double-tap the Home button to bring up the multitasking panel. This displays your open apps and allows you to switch between them.

2 Select apps Slide your finger to the right to find an app you want to load.

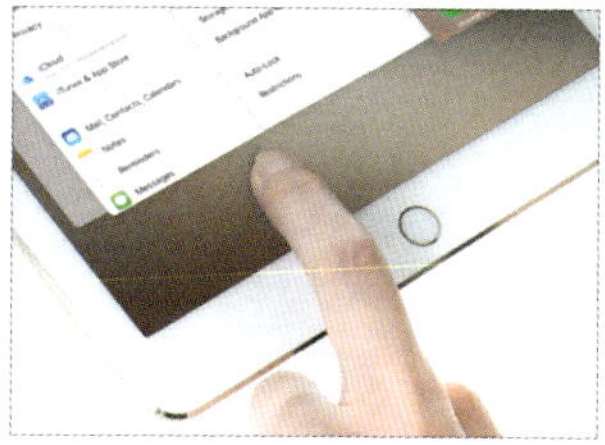

3 Close it You can close the app with a flick up from the multitasking screen.

Manage your apps

1 The Home screen To navigate the Home screen you will mostly use the swipe gesture to switch between multiple screens of icons. Simply swipe to the left to see the next screen and to the right to return to the first.

2 Tap and drag Tap and hold on an app and drag it around to move it.

3 Folders Drag one app over another to create an app folder.

Change the volume with headphones

1 Small buttons When the headphones are attached to the iPad, press the volume keys on the headphone cable.

2 Visual notifications You will see the volume level move on the screen as you press the buttons.

Use the Multitasking feature

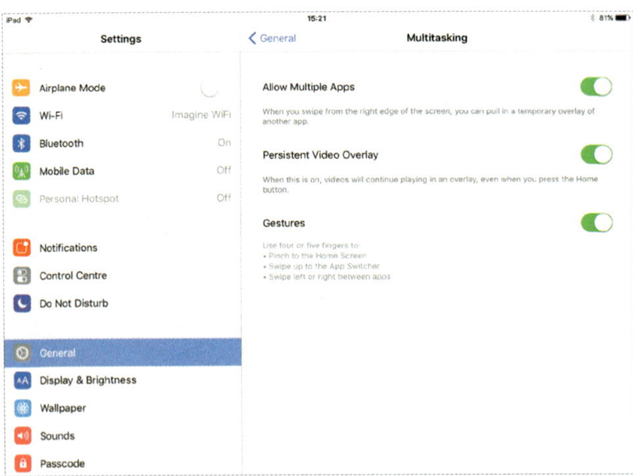

1 Turn it on In order to use Multitasking while using other apps, you must go into Settings>General>Multitasking and make sure you have toggled on Allow Multiple Apps. Now you'll be able to use split screen.

2 Swipe right While in an app, swipe over from the right-hand side.

3 View app Tap on the app you want to see and it will appear on the right.

Mute your iPad

1 The Mute button Slide the small button above the volume to reveal a red marker. This will mute the iPad, which can be useful to stop alerts. The iPad Air 2 doesn't have this button, so you can mute the device through the Control Centre.

2 Use the keys Hold the volume down button to mute.

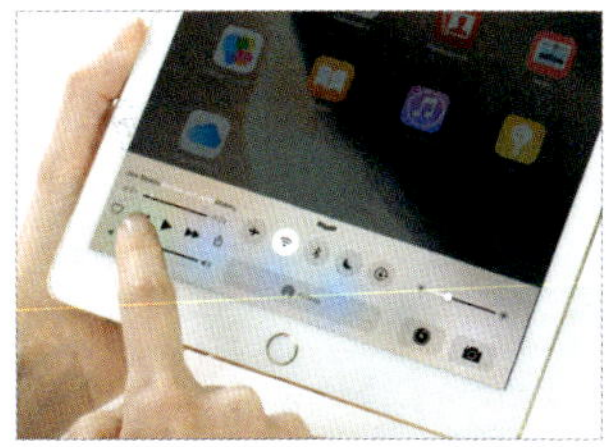

3 Control Centre gives you quick access to the volume gauge.

Set the rotation lock

1 Control Centre Flick up to launch Control Centre and then select the rotation lock icon.

2 The Mute button In Settings> General you can set the Side Switch to lock the rotation.

3 Landscape as well You are able to lock the rotation in both portrait and landscape modes.

Set the brightness

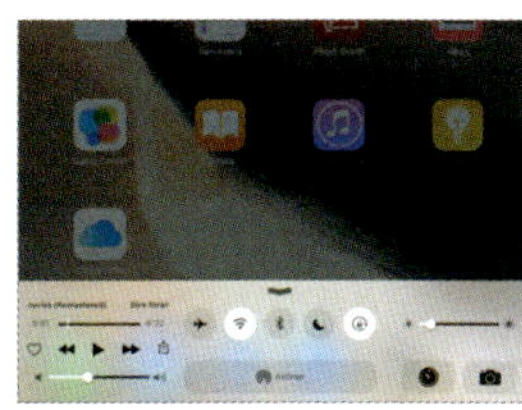

1 Use slider You can also find a shortcut to adjust your iPad's output in the Control Centre.

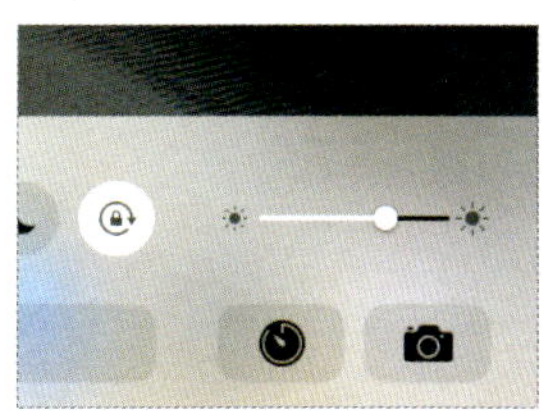

2 Slide for brightness Move the slider left and right to adjust the brightness down and up.

Hand gestures on your iPad

Learn the many ways you can control your iPad using the power of your fingers

Fig 1, Tap You will need to tap to launch apps

Fig 2, Scroll Drag your finger to navigate around

Fig 3, Swipe Use this gesture to switch pages

Fig 4, Drag Keep your finger held down

Fig 5, Pinch Use this gesture to zoom out

1 **Tap** Tapping is the main way you will navigate your iPad. To open an app, you must tap it from your Home screen, for example (Fig 1). You'll mainly be tapping the iPad to select things like web links in Safari, songs in Music, or pictures in Photos. You'll also need to tap to type on the on-screen keyboard when it appears in numerous apps such as Mail, Messages, Reminders and Notes.

2 **Scroll** Scrolling is when you drag your finger up or down the iPad's screen (Fig 2). This is most useful when the iPad can't fit all the information on one screen, so you need to slide your finger up to move the screen down and vice versa. This is most common in apps like Safari, Notes and, depending on the size of your collections, Music and Videos.

3 **Swipe** Where scrolling is vertical, swiping is horizontal – you just need to move your finger from left to right or vice versa. Once you start filling your iPad up with apps, you'll need to swipe to switch between pages of apps on the Home screen (Fig 3). It's also needed to flick through the pages of your ebooks in iBooks and your magazines in Newsstand.

4 **Drag** Dragging is when you tap and hold your finger on the iPad, then drag it anywhere else on the screen. It's essential when moving apps around on the Home screen. Tap and hold on an app until all other apps start wobbling. You can now drag it to its rightful place on the Home screen. It's rarely used in other native apps, but common in third-party games.

5 **Pinch** Widely used among built-in and third-party apps, the pinch is a very useful gesture. To perform it, place two fingers on the screen and bring them together (Fig 5). It won't do anything on the Home screen, but in many apps, including Photos and Maps, it zooms out the display. The more distance between your two fingers, the larger the zoom.

6 **Spread** The spread is essentially the opposite to the pinch: rather than bringing two digits together, you spread them apart (Fig 6). The effect is also the opposite, as rather than zooming out, you zoom in instead. This is particularly useful in Safari, when perhaps you need to zoom in to read particularly small text; or Photos, when you want to inspect an image close-up.

Enable Multitasking Gestures by going to Settings, then General, and tapping the slider

7 Five-finger pinch After enabling Multitasking Gestures in the General section of Settings, you will be able to perform a four or five-finger pinch. This works in most apps, and it will automatically take you back to the Home screen. To perform the pinch, place all five fingers on the iPad screen and then bring them all towards a single point (Fig 7).

8 Five-finger scroll To access your recently used apps quickly, place all five fingers on the iPad screen and then move them all upwards (Fig 8). This will reveal the multitasking bar. From here you can choose a recently used app to use by tapping on it. If you tap and hold the app you will be able to remove it from the multitasking bar by tapping the red icon.

9 Five-finger swipe left/right To switch between apps quickly, place all your fingers on the iPad, then move from right to left (Fig 9). This gesture enables you to switch quickly between your current app and last used app without bringing up the multitasking bar. You don't get a selection of apps to choose from, so it's most useful when frequently moving between two apps.

10 Three-finger double-tap To enable these next three gestures, you must activate them by going into the Settings app, tapping on Accessibility and then choosing Zoom. Once enabled, if you double-tap the screen with three fingers you will zoom into the screen (Fig 10), similar to the Spread gesture. However, this gesture can be done anywhere – including the Home screen.

11 Three-finger scroll When you're zoomed in with a three-finger double-tap, you can navigate around the screen by tapping and holding three fingers on the iPad and scrolling with them. This enables you to navigate around a zoomed app (or the Home screen) while still letting you use normal gestures (such as Tap and Swipe) to operate the app.

12 Three-finger drag The regular three-finger double-tap zoom is binary: it's either zoomed or it's not. To change the level of zoom, double-tap the iPad with three fingers again, but hold your fingers down after the second tap. Now scroll up or down to change the level of zoom. No matter how far you zoom in, a three-finger double-tap will bring you back to where you were.

Fig 6, Spread Use this gesture to zoom in

Fig 7, Five-finger pinch Use this to go Home

Fig 8, Five-finger scroll up Access multitasking

Fig 9, Five-finger swipe Use this to switch apps

Fig 10, Three-finger double-tap Enable it first

Applications

An at-a-glance guide to what Apple's built-in apps and App Store products can do for you

Fig 1, Settings Personalise your iPad

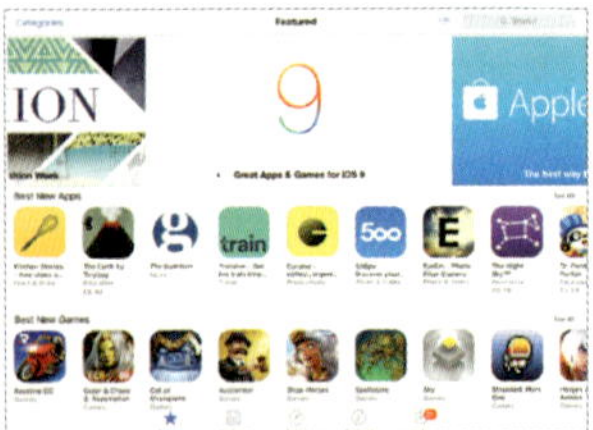

Fig 2, App Store Home to over 750,000 apps

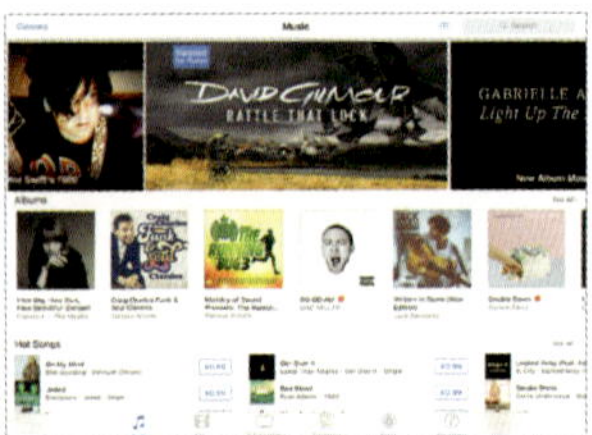

Fig 3, iTunes Your online entertainment store

Fig 4, Music It's easy to listen to tunes in Music

Fig 5, Safari Browsing with tabs in Safari

Settings This is where you'll be able to change how your iPad works. You can connect to Wi-Fi, passcode-protect your device, and update the software, among many other things – all from this app. See page 32.

App Store Although the built-in apps on your iPad are fantastic and will benefit your life in many different ways, you can download and buy more apps from Apple's built-in App Store. See page 44.

iTunes Through this service you can download the hottest new albums and films, all from the comfort of your sofa. Just search for what you want, tap to buy and you'll have it in minutes. See page 48.

Music Through this app you can listen to all of your purchased iTunes music, or music that you've transferred to your iPad. You can also enjoy Apple Music, the new streaming service. See page 52.

Videos All of the TV shows and movies that you've downloaded from iTunes, along with any that you've transferred from your computer, will be viewable through this simple but effective app. See page 56.

Safari This app is the best way to browse the internet on your iPad. Provided you're connected to Wi-Fi, you can use Safari to surf the web with tabs, browse privately or add items to read offline. See page 60.

Mail Round-the-clock access to your email account is vital in today's world. Your iPad's Mail app helps you achieve this with an easy setup process and an intuitive interface. See page 64.

Calendar If you need to organise your life, then check out this app. It enables you to set up events, schedule appointments and basically take control of your day, week, month or even year! See page 68.

Contacts Keep in touch with everyone with the iPad's built-in address book. On the iPhone, find your contacts within Phone, or add the Contacts app on the Home screen from the Utilities folder. See page 72.

Messages Send a text message on your iPhone, or on your iPad you can take advantage of iMessage – a free messaging service that enables you to text users with other iOS devices. See page 76.

Reminders If you find yourself regularly forgetting to do various tasks, use the Reminders app to give you a nudge. Set priorities and the exact times at which you need to be reminded. See page 80.

Notes Revamped for iOS 9, with notes you can now create quick and easy to-do lists, add content from other sources and even scribble new notes down using your finger. See page 82.

Maps This app will help you keep track of where you are in the world. It'll give you directions and show you how bad the traffic situation is, among many other things. See page 84.

FaceTime Of course your iPad can't make a phone call, but it doesn't need to – it has FaceTime! Chat face-to-face with someone on another iOS device for free using a Wi-Fi connection. See page 88.

Camera It may surprise you, but your iPad is capable of taking some very good pictures – especially the newer models. So use the exceptional built-in Camera app to your advantage. See page 90.

Photos Once you've taken your photos or videos, you'll need a place to view them. Luckily, the Photos app is the perfect place for you to marvel at your images, and even make edits to them. See page 94.

News A new app for iOS 9, News replaces the Newsstand app for all of your digital magazines and provides a handy one-stop news digest for all of your favourite news sources. See page 100.

iBooks If you fancy reading something a bit more traditional on your iPad, then check out iBooks and the iBook Store for thousands of ebooks, which can all be read the way you want. See page 104.

Game Center Take advantage of the millions of games available on your iPad with Game Center. The app tracks your achievements and has leaderboards for many of the top games on iOS. See page 108.

iCloud Drive The new iCloud Drive is a robust and reliable cloud storage service that enables you to store all of your documents, images, and more, whenever you need them. See page 112.

iMovie If you want to turn your iPad movies into something special, look no further. You can cut trailers, add special effects, and turn your family into the stars of professional-looking films. See page 114.

Pages This app turns your iPad into an amazing mobile word processor. You can create documents on the go in style by downloading Pages from the App Store. See page 120.

Numbers This is an intuitive app, made by Apple and available from the App Store, that helps you create spreadsheets and present your data in a format that's easy to understand. See page 124.

Keynote Perfect for creating your own professional slideshow presentations, Keynote is a fantastically easy-to-use app that will make your information much more appealing. See page 126.

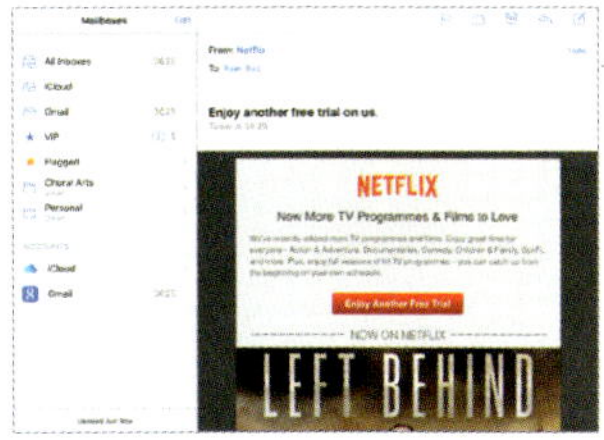

Fig 6, Mail Organise your emails with ease

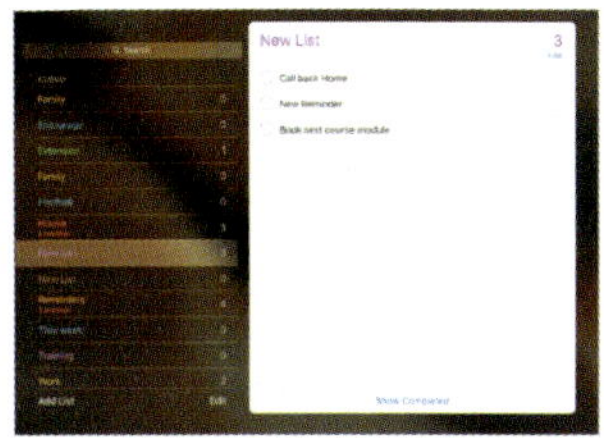

Fig 7, Reminders Never forget anything again

Fig 8, Maps Use Maps to find your way

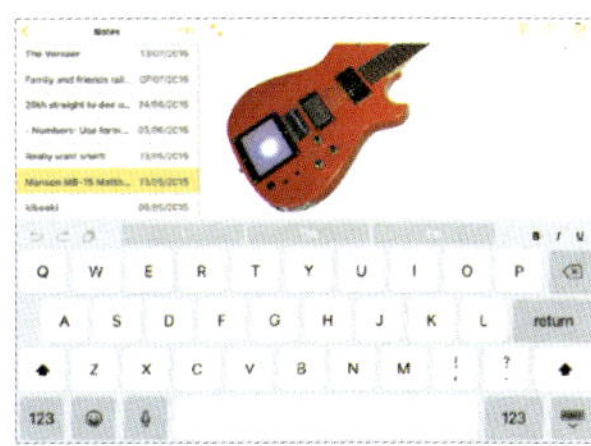

Fig 9, Notes Easier to use and more versatile

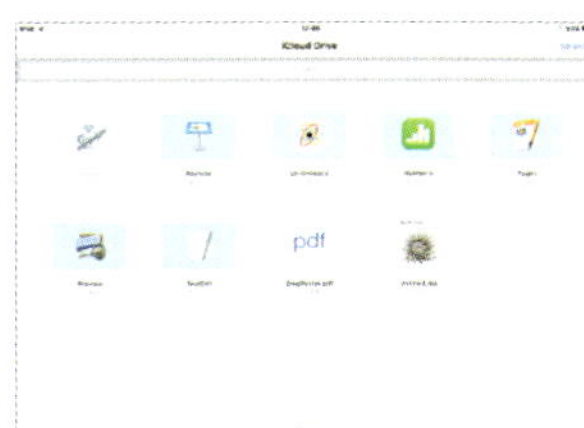

Fig 10, iCloud Drive Sync your files wirelessly

Settings

We provide you with a guided tour around the nerve centre of your iPad

You'll use it to...

Connect to the internet
Establish a Wi-Fi connection to your device

Manage notifications
Determine how your iOS 9 device alerts you to various things

Personalise your iPad
Change the wallpaper, accessibility of your device and much more

Manage your iCloud
Connect to your cloud, and manage your storage and backup

Enable restrictions
Passcode-protect your device and set age restrictions on apps

Get social
Log into your Twitter and Facebook accounts to integrate them into your apps

Take control of your iPad

The Settings app, which you can launch by tapping its icon on the Home screen, is where you can tailor the functionality of your iPad to suit your needs, as well as personalise its appearance and services. In Settings, the categories are laid out in the left-hand column, freeing up the right-hand side to display the options (Fig 1).

Notification Centre

Your iPad is constantly alerting you to new things – incoming emails, messages, Game Center friend requests and other assorted app alerts – and Notification Centre lets you keep track of them easily by accessing a handy drop-down panel. To access your Notification Centre, you swipe down from the top of the screen and all of your recent notifications will be displayed in a list.

To tailor your Notification Centre to your own specific needs, launch the Settings app and then tap on the Notifications section from the main Settings list. The main screen presents a list of apps

Fig 1 (above) In the Settings app, the functions are listed on the left and the options on the right

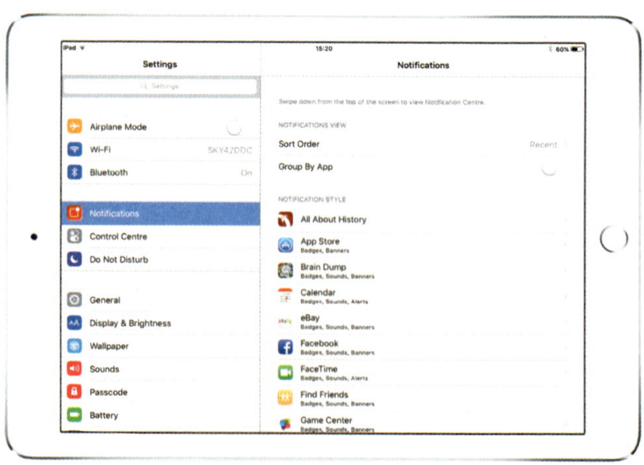

Fig 2 (right) Tap 'Edit' in your Notifications settings and press and hold on the list icon next to an app to change the order

that are in your Notification Centre (and a list of those that are not, which you can add to the list). By tapping the Edit button in the top-right corner you can move apps between lists and change the order of how the apps appear in your Notification Centre (Fig 2). To determine how your iPad receives alerts, tap on an app in the list and you can set the style of alert and also whether or not it will flash up on your Lock screen. See the Notification Centre section of this bookazine for more information.

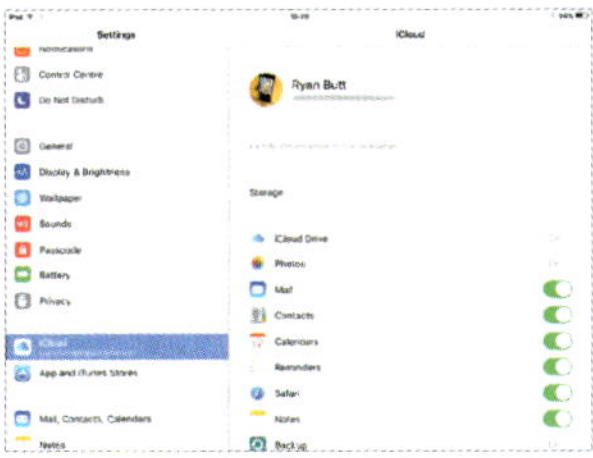

iCloud

Apple's iCloud service is free to use and stores your music, photos, documents and more, and wirelessly sends them to all of your iOS devices without you having to manually transfer files. This service has grown with the release of iOS 9 and now several new features have been added. Family Sharing allows up to six family members to share purchases from iTunes and the App Store and also provides options to pay for your family's digital purchases from the same credit card and approve the purchases of your kids from your device. The Keychain feature lets you save all of your passwords and personal details in the cloud and use them on any device and iCloud Drive is a place where you can store all of your documents and files and not only access them on any device, but also pick files from one app to open in another app. In short iOS 9 is a cloud revolution.

Back up your iPad

As you will have all sorts of important stuff on your iPad, iCloud will provide peace of mind by automatically backing up your device daily over Wi-Fi when your device is connected to a power source.

Manage your iCloud storage by tapping on the 'Storage' option in the iCloud settings

Connect to the internet via Wi-Fi

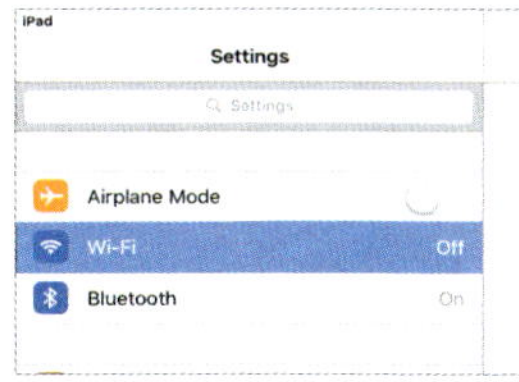

1 Go to Wi-Fi Settings
In Settings, tap on Wi-Fi and ensure that the slider is turned on.

2 Choose network
Your device will scan for networks. Tap on a Wi-Fi network to select it.

3 Enter password
You'll be prompted to enter your password. Do so, then tap 'Join'.

4 Connected
A tick will indicate that you are connected to your network.

Settings

Fig 3 Ensure all of your essential data is backed up in the background by enabling the iCloud Backup option

Once you plug it in, everything is backed up without you having to lift a finger. When you set up a new iDevice or need to restore the information on one you already have, iCloud does all the heavy lifting for you. Just connect your device to Wi-Fi, enter your Apple ID, and then all your purchased music, TV shows, books and apps, will appear on your device. To activate this service, launch your Settings app and tap on the iCloud section. Next, tap on the Backup option in the list if iCloud services and ensure iCloud Backup is turned on. All of your data will be backed up when your iPad is plugged in, locked and connected to Wi-Fi. You can also back it up immediately by tapping on the 'Back Up Now' option (Fig 3). While you are in the iCloud settings, also be sure to turn on the 'Keychain' option so that all of your credit card info and passwords are stored in the cloud.

Software update
If a number is shown next to your General settings it means that a Software Update is available. Tap this option to find out more

Your iCloud account
Your iCloud account is tied in with your iTunes account that you have set up on your device to purchase media and apps

Available storage
Tap on the Storage & Backup option to review how much of your cloud you are using and buy more space, if necessary

Compatible apps
All of the apps that incorporate iCloud will be presented in a list. Move the sliders to the On position to activate their respective iCloud features

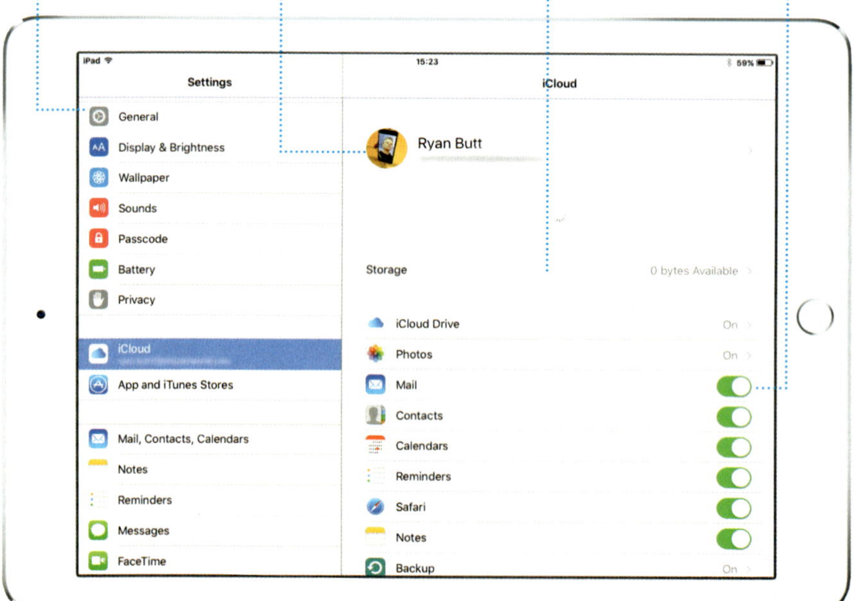

Under the General Settings, tap on 'Software Update' to search for possible iOS updates

Change the wallpaper

If you want to change the appearance of your iPad then you can do so under the new 'Wallpaper' option in Settings (in iOS 9 the Display & Brightness settings now have their own standalone section). To change the wallpaper, tap on the 'Choose a New Wallpaper' option and you will be presented with three sections to tap on. The first, called Dynamic, allows you to choose from a selection of pre-loaded animated wallpapers. The second option, Stills, provides a selection of still images that are already installed on your device and the third, called Photos, lets you fashion a background out of a photograph in your Photos app. Whichever option you choose, tap on your selection and it will be displayed full-screen. Now simply tap either the Set Lock screen or Set Home screen buttons to instantly set the image as your chosen backdrop on either your Lock screen or your Home screen. Alternatively, tap on the Set Both option to use the same image for both screens.

Enable parental restrictions

As you have invested quite a significant sum of money in your iPad, as well as the various apps and iTunes media content that you have

Customise Spotlight

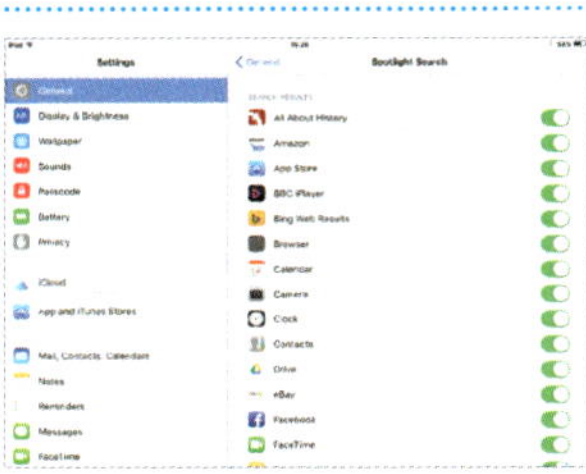

1 Go to Spotlight Search Settings
In General Settings, tap Spotlight Search and pick the apps to include.

2 Initiate a search
On your Home screen, swipe down to access the Spotlight Search feature.

Set keyboard shortcuts

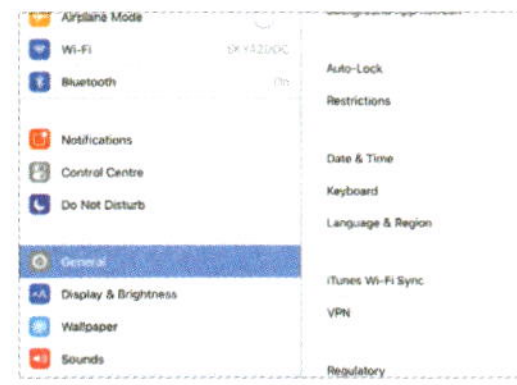

1 Access keyboard settings
In the Settings app, tap on General and then Keyboard.

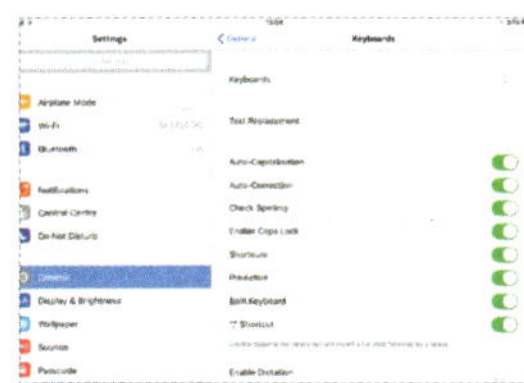

2 Enable shortcuts
Move the shortcut sliders to 'On' to enable the various features.

3 Adding shortcuts
Tap on 'Text Replacement' to start adding your own by tapping '+'.

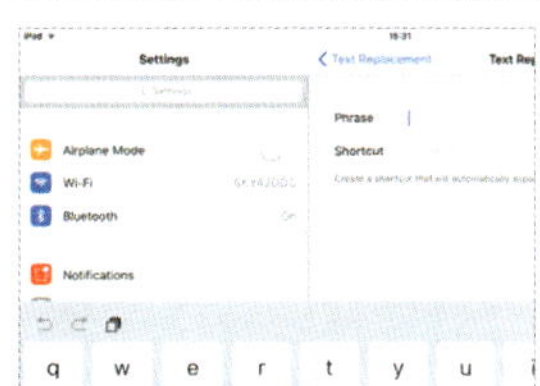

4 Creating shortcuts
Type in a word or phrase followed by the shortcut you wish to use.

To prevent other users buying apps, go to General>Restrictions> Password Settings

bought, you will naturally want to impose restrictions on who can access your material. Likewise, if your device is shared throughout the family then enabling restrictions will mean that inappropriate material cannot be accessed through the device and expensive apps can't be purchased by accident.

To start enabling restrictions, go to the General Settings section and then tap on Restrictions. By tapping on the Enable Restrictions option at the top of the page, you will first be required to enter a four-digit passcode. Do so and then move the sliders to the On position for the apps that may be accessed and then review the list of allowed content. To impose greater restrictions, go back to the General page and tap on Passcode Lock.

Explore your Privacy settings

If you value your privacy then you may have already explored your iPad's privacy settings and have things set up exactly how you want them. However, if you have only recently upgraded your iPad's firmware to iOS 9 then new settings will come into play and your original settings may have been reset. Tap on the Privacy section and then tap on Location Services. This screen displays the apps

Impose restrictions

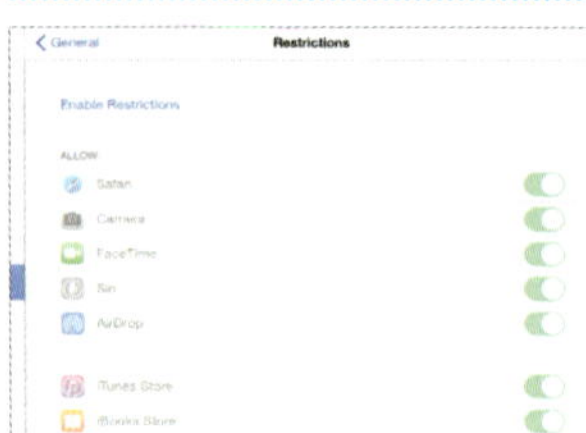

1 Tap on Restrictions
In the General Settings page, tap on the Restrictions section.

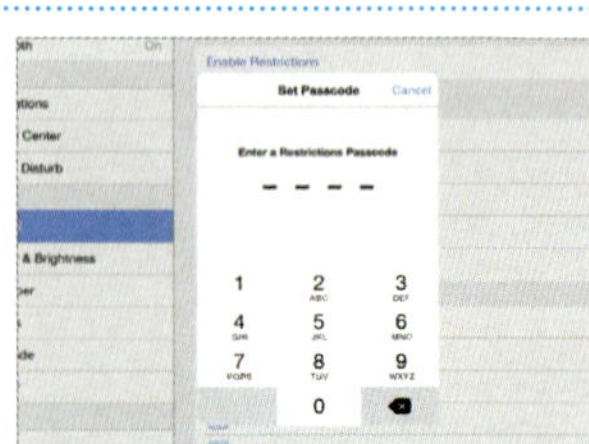

2 Enable restrictions
Tap on Enable Restrictions and then set a four-digit passcode.

Set a passcode

1 Tap Passcode
In the Settings app, tap on the new standalone Passcode option.

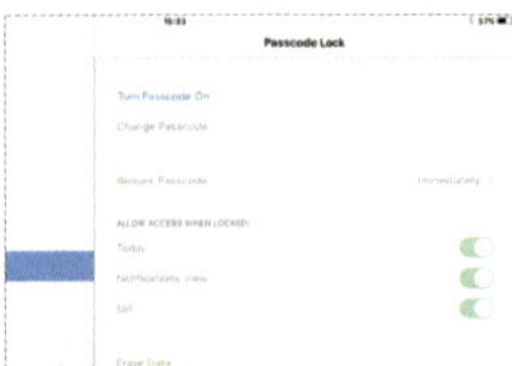

2 Turn it on
Tap on the Turn Passcode On option at the top of the page.

3 Enter a code
Enter and confirm a four-digit code to protect your device.

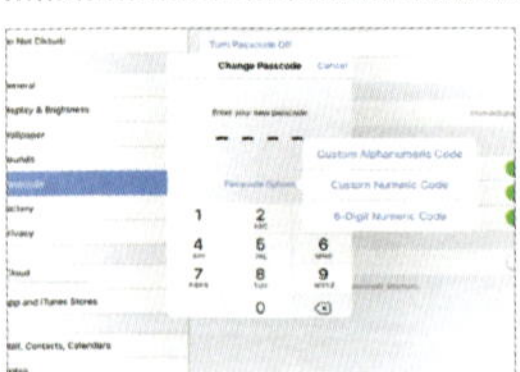

4 Secure passcode
Tap 'Passcode Options' to select a different, more secure code.

that you have permitted to track your location. Featured on this screen will be a list of the apps that have been granted permission to track your location (Fig 4). Consider if certain apps really need to know where you are or require location data to work properly and turn them off if you deduce they don't need it (this will help conserve your battery power too).

Also, back out to the main Privacy screen and scroll down to see two curious options – Diagnostics & Usage and Advertising. Diagnostics & Usage sends info on what you do on your iPad to Apple to help improve services so do you want that enabled? Probably not. Now tap on the Advertising option and consider limiting the amount of usage information that is sent to Apple and its partners to gauge your position and tailor ads accordingly. Again, knowing what options you need and don't need to use can help ensure that your device's battery lasts noticeably longer.

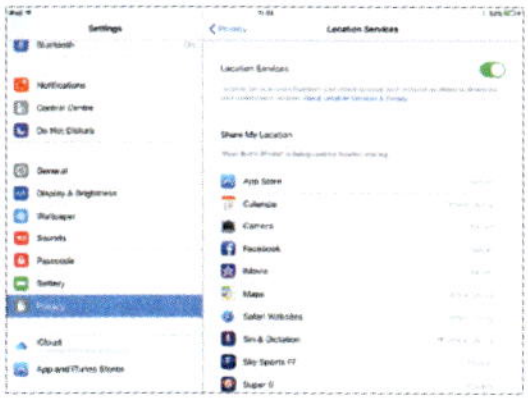

Fig 4 Tap on Location Services to view all of the apps that currently have access to your location. You can turn them off here

Passcode Lock
Activate this feature to protect your device from unwanted users. You can set a four-digit code or something more complicated

Lock rotation
Sick of your iPad screen flipping between portrait and landscape when you accidentally tilt your device? Then lock it here

Keyboard
You can set the keyboard up to be both easier to use and quicker to type by adjusting the various Keyboard settings

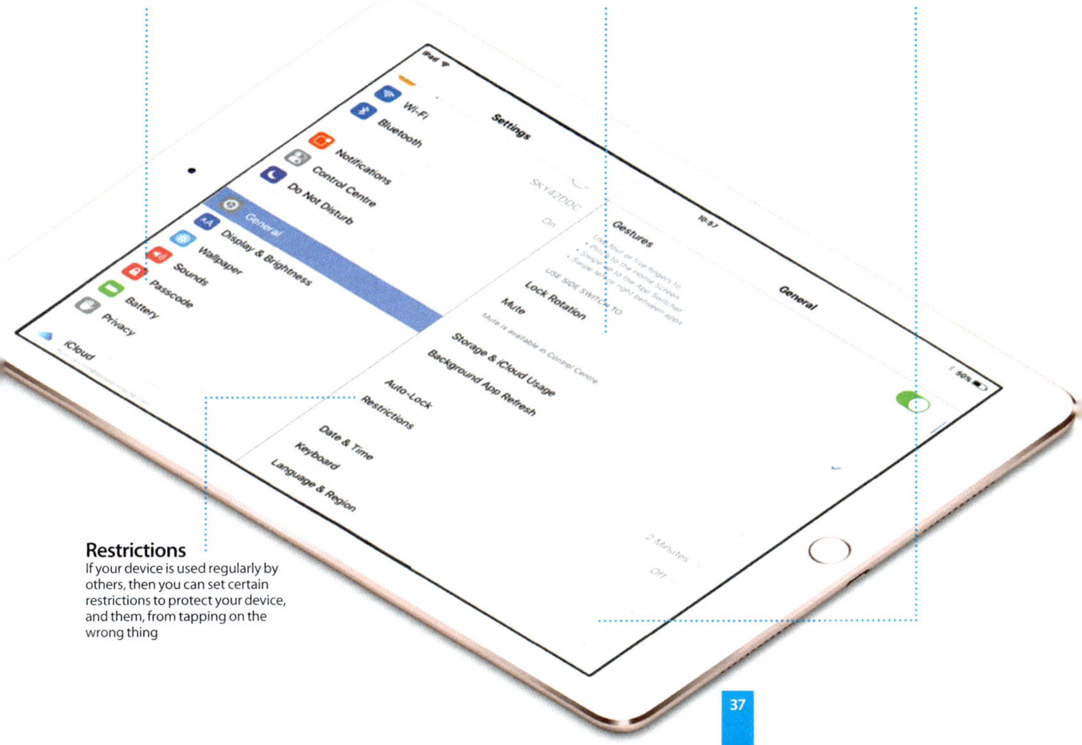

Restrictions
If your device is used regularly by others, then you can set certain restrictions to protect your device, and them, from tapping on the wrong thing

Notification Centre

Notification Centre allows you to view your daily events and any alerts that pop-up within the system

You'll use it to...

View your calendar events
Calendar events, including a snapshot of tomorrow's schedule can be viewed via the Notification Centre

Launch your calendar
Viewed events can be selected to launch the Calendar app

View app alerts
Any apps that send notifications will be listed in the All section

Launch apps
Similarly app alerts can be selected to launch the chosen app or function

View missed calls
Any missed calls (including FaceTime) will be listed here

Customise notifications
You can use the Home>Settings option to customise your Notifications

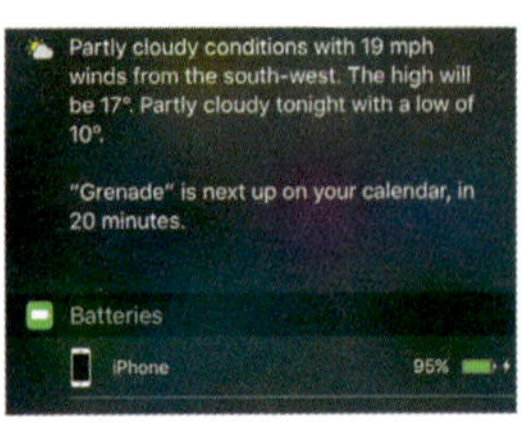

Fig 1 (above) Notification Centre is useful to display Calendar events, notification alerts, weather and battery status

Fig 2 (right) The Notification Centre can be activated by swiping down from the top of the screen

Stay up to date

The Notification Centre, when configured properly, can be a useful tool. It allows you to view your calendar events for the day and a brief snapshot of any scheduled events tomorrow. Additionally you can view any third-party app alerts such as a connect message in Twitter, or you can view any missed calls or text messages.

View your notifications

By default you have several visual clues when notifications come in to your device. Usually you will get an audible ping followed by a snapshot of the alert at the top of your screen. Alternatively a further reminder will take the shape of a red circle in the upper corner of your app icon. This will usually indicate a new notification. You can then view a larger overview of the notifications by swiping down

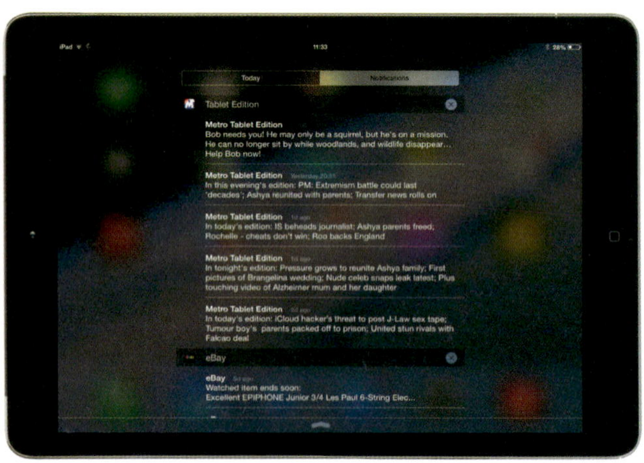

from the top of the screen (this can be initiated from any app and the Lock screen). In iOS 9 notifications are split into two tabs in the Notification Centre. The first is 'Today', which showcases current calendar events, while the 'Notifications tab' lists any third-party app notifications, alongside a brief description of the notification (you can tap the notification to launch the respective app). A third tab, 'Missed' will be added in the event of any missed phone and FaceTime calls.

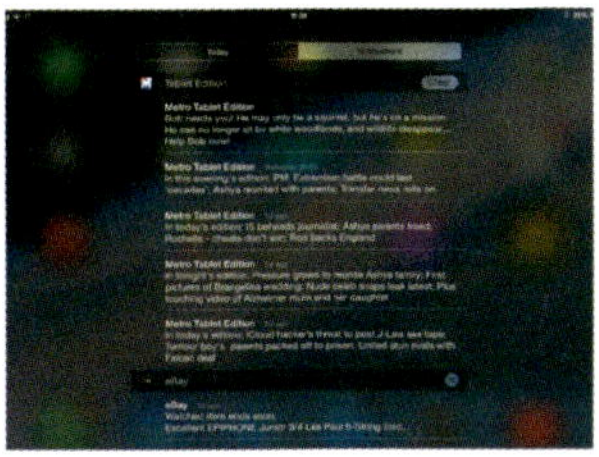

Remove notifications

When dealing with newly installed third-party apps, every app will always ask you whether it can send push notifications to your device before you head fully into the app's interface. If you decline, this will of course stop you from getting any more alerts, but for the notifications that are still present, the Notification Centre makes life even easier to remove them. On your iPad you simply need to swipe down the Notification Centre and tap on the 'X' in the right-hand corner of each set of notifications. Choose Clear to remove them.

Change Notification Centre settings

If you want to adjust how notifications are handled, you can do so by heading to Home>Settings> Notifications. From here you can control the Lock screen settings, how calendar events will be displayed and how your notifications will be sorted. Under the Include section you'll see the apps that currently support the Notification function and you can select these apps to disable them. Similarly, under the Do Not Include section you can enable any apps.

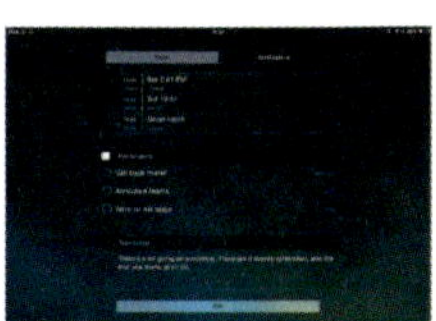

Instead of tapping on the Notification tabs you can use a swipe motion to access the options

Change alert styles

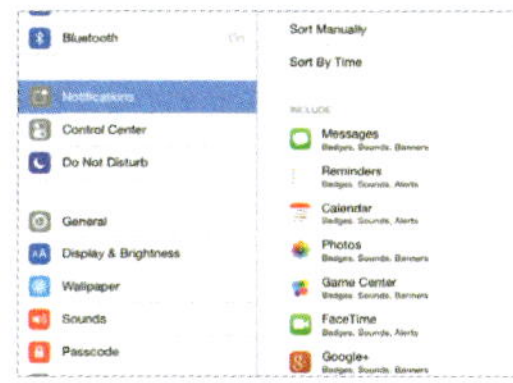

1 Notification Centre settings
From the Home screen head to Settings>Notifications.

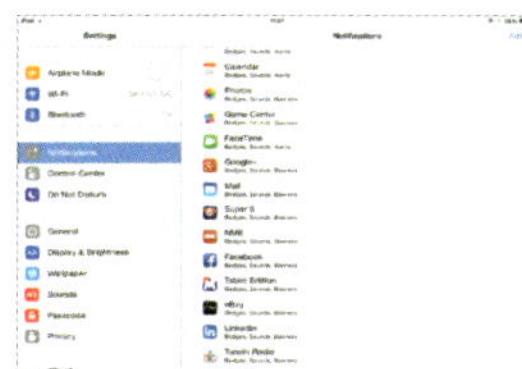

2 Select the app
Select your app from under the Include section.

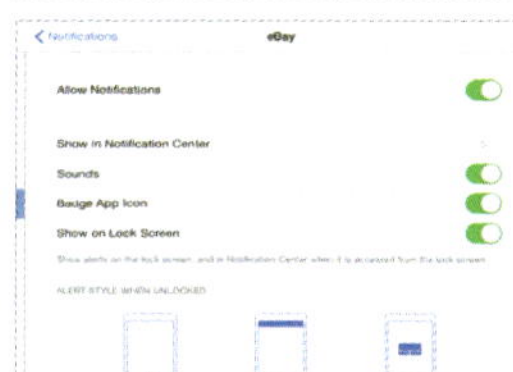

3 Slider options
At the top you can also adjust Badge App Icon and Sounds.

4 Adjust additional options
You can also choose a notification style for your alert.

Control Centre

The Control Centre provides you with an instant array of essential commands

You'll use it to...

Control playback
Select music and change the volume

Connect with AirPlay
Establish a connection between your iPad and other compatible devices

Take a quick picture
Access the Camera instantly

Switch on Airplane Mode
Make your iPad safe for air travel by turning off Wi-Fi and more

Access Alarm & Timer
Set your time preferences

Quickly access multiple tools

Control Centre is an instant commands centre. That is, Apple has collected all of those tools that you need 'now', allowing you to access them without faffing around with menu trees and other complications. Control Centre gives you instant access.

Set up Control Centre

If there was a problem with the earlier version of the iOS operating system, it was how many of the frequently accessed features were often buried within the deeper reaches of the Settings. With the Control Centre, Apple has made many common tasks available right from the Home screen, making them directly accessible by swiping the menu from the bottom of the screen via a translucent layer, providing quick access to a host of settings and functions.

To set up the Control Centre, tap the Settings icon then locate the Control Centre function on the left pane and tap on it. You can access the Control Centre options when you are at the Lock screen

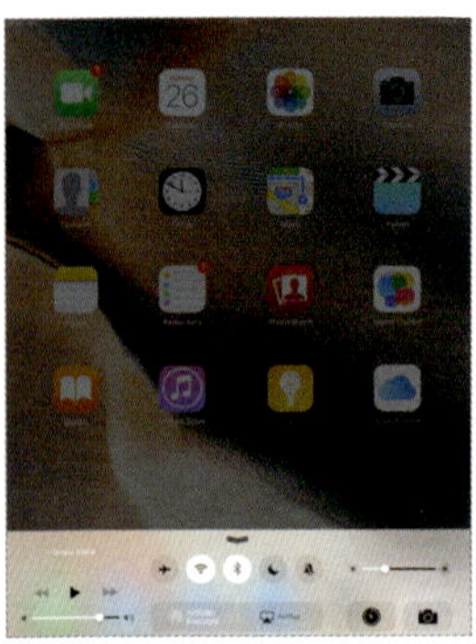

Fig 1 (above) The Control Centre collects essential tools into one, quick-access space

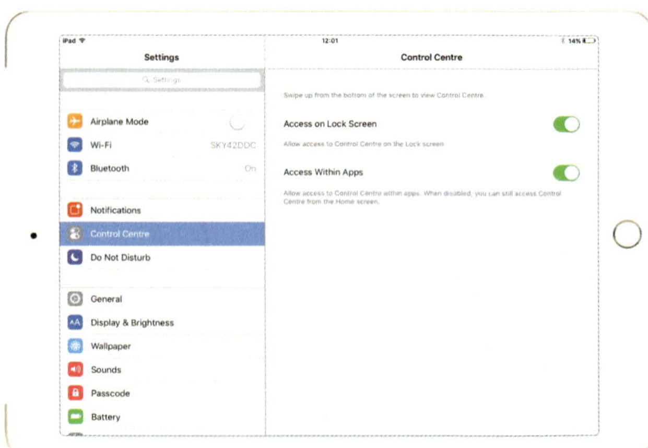

Fig 2 (right) Access services instantly with essential controls at your fingertips

stage. Swipe the 'Access on Lock Screen' button to green. Swipe the Access Within Apps button to green to access the Control Centre with your Apps, valuable when you want to access a service directly. Swipe the Access Within Apps option to the left and Off to remove the Control Centre option. This is useful when playing games.

Play and control music

Activate the Control Centre via the Home screen or, if allowed, from within an app. View the Control Centre by swiping upwards with a single finger from the base of the screen. The Centre takes up a small portion of the screen. To the left of the Control Centre is a suite of media controls used to control played music or video images in a traditional play/pause and fast forward/reverse fashion. The base of the Control Centre features two slider controls. The left controls the volume and the right controls the brightness. Slide each control to increase and reduce the levels.

Manage communications and accessories

The central bank of circled commands are push button functions, shining white when active. Among these is Airplane Mode, which turns off all potentially harmful functions, such as Wi-Fi, when on a commercial airline. Speaking of Wi-Fi, you can also turn this option on or off too. In the same family of functions, you can also toggle the Bluetooth facility. You may need to toggle these functions in a public place immediately when requested, so this sort of instant access is necessary. For different reasons, the Do Not Disturb feature might be something you access when you are concentrating on something else or about to get some sleep. Instant access is appreciated in this case.

Tap the Orientation lock button in Control Centre to toggle screen orientation on or off

Access the clock app

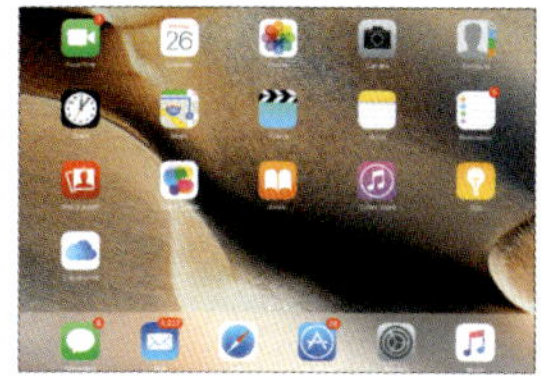

1 Clock and alarms
Start the iPad or go to the Home or app screen.

2 Trigger Control Centre
Swipe the Control Centre from the base of the screen upwards.

3 Access clock icon
Locate the Clock/alarm app icon at the right of the Control Centre.

4 Use Clock app
Set your alarm or view your desired world clock mode.

Siri

An intelligent voice-controlled command system that uses artificial intelligence facilities

You'll use it to...

Control apps
Go hands-free by using your voice to operate your iPad

Search the internet
Initiate a web search with simple speech

Set functions
Operate utilities such as alarms or clocks

Get productive
Access and run creative apps quickly and easily with just your voice

Receive directions
Ask Siri to locate and direct you to wherever you want to go

Communicate with friends
Use Siri to update social media

Teach Siri about you

Siri enables you to control your iPad with your voice – but to improve its performance, you'll need to teach the app more about you. Tap on Settings then General. Locate Siri and tap on it. Make sure that Siri is switched to the green (On) position then tap My Info (Fig 1). Select your contact information from the list.

Search the web

To initiate the Siri app, press the Home button long enough for the app to start or simply say, "Hey Siri". Siri will begin with a question: "What can I help you with?" If you don't respond quickly enough, it will click into demo mode, showing "Some things you can ask me." This is actually a useful series of screens that provide a selection of the sort of questions that you can ask the app. When you are ready to speak, tap on the microphone and the app will beep in response. Decide upon your web search question. In this case, we will search for a bread recipe. And that's what we will say: "Search for bread

Fig 1 (above) Enhance Siri's overall performance by providing it with your personal information

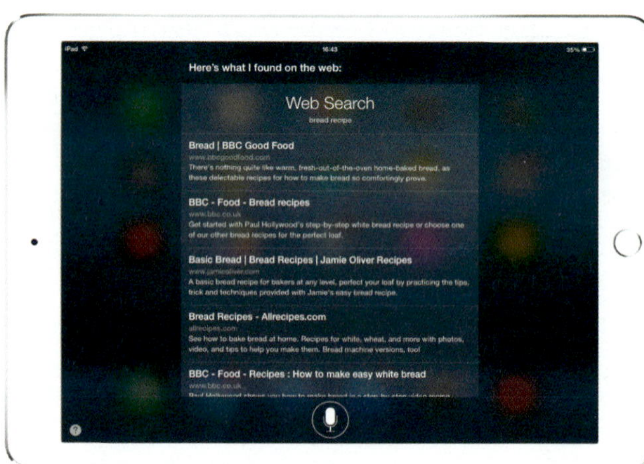

Fig 2 (right) Your verbal search commands will produce web-based results on the Siri screen

recipe." A list of recipes will fill the screen, directly from the web (Fig 2). In most cases, this being one, you will be able to scroll to see more results and also related images. In addition to the images, you may also see a selection of videos which you can tap to play, plus related search titles which can provide additional results.

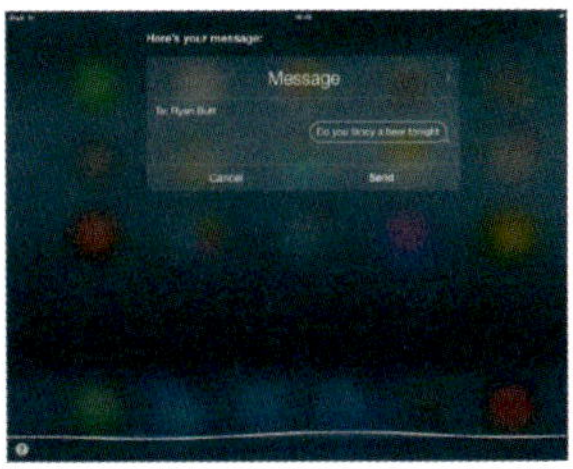

Speak your text message

Sending a text message manually can be quite a time-intensive operation involving a selection of menu choices. Alternatively, Siri offers one series of vocal commands to speed up the operation. Press the Home button until Siri appears on the screen or say "Hey Siri" to get started. Tap on the microphone. Say: "Send a text message," and Siri will ask for a recipient. This will have to be someone present in your Contacts book. Provide a name then provide the content by speaking the message itself. You can either tap on the Send button on the screen or say: "Send text message," to conclude the task.

Update your social networks

It seemed inevitable, with iOS becoming so integrated with Twitter, that Siri would follow suit. Using Siri, you can interact with the popular social-media service. If your proposed contact is resident on your Contacts section and has a Twitter address, you can contact them via Siri within Twitter. You can also find tweets with a specific hashtag. So, for example, say: "Find tweets with the hashtag LiverpoolFC," to find messages relating to the football team. Interacting with Facebook is more limited as Siri doesn't search this service, but it will post social-network updates for you. Just say: "Post to Facebook," followed by what you want your friends to know.

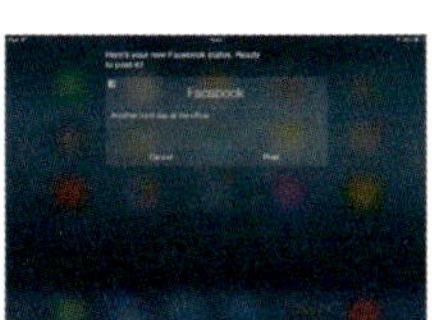

Say: "Write on my wall," to make Siri compose and post a status update to your Facebook page

Find a restaurant

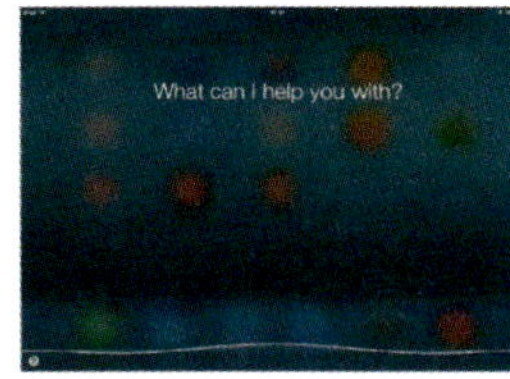

1 Start Siri
Press the Home key until Siri starts up or say "Hey Siri".

2 Search for restaurants
A selection of restaurants close to your location is listed.

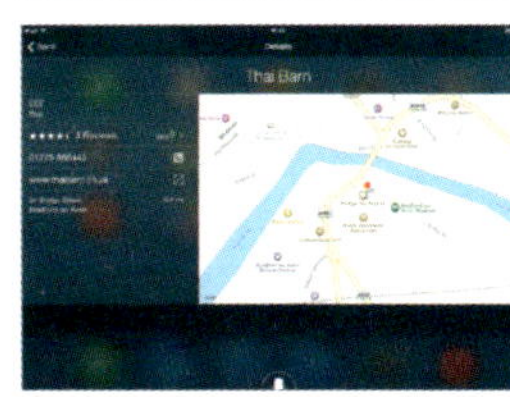

3 Detailed information
Ask Siri for more information on your desired restaurant.

4 Request directions
Siri will take you to Maps, providing you with directions.

App Store

Your gateway to a rich source of apps is via the intuitive App Store – a bustling marketplace that is always open for business

You'll use it to…

Discover apps
Clearly defined sections help you find and discover exciting new apps

Search for apps
If you know the name of an app, enter it in the search field and you'll find it in seconds

Purchase apps
Buy and download apps to your device

Gift apps
Send an app to someone special

Review apps
Give a little customer feedback

Get recommendations
Use the Near Me feature to see what apps are popular around you

Shop for apps

The App Store will be your most-used iOS device app because it is here that you purchase and download content for your device (Fig 1). Thankfully, it is a very user-friendly environment where you can discover what's hot and make informed purchases in seconds.

Search the App Store

Considering that the shelves of the App Store have swelled to over 900,000 products, with 375,000 specifically for iPad, being able to find what you need quickly is of the ultimate importance – so it's just as well that there is an intuitive search engine on hand to help.

If you know the name of the app you're looking for then enter it into the Search field (Fig 2). As you type the letters, matches will instantly start being made with what you're typing. If you see what you want in the list of suggestions, then just tap on it to instantly go

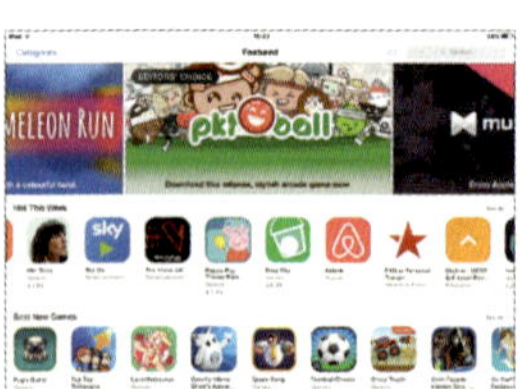

Fig 1 (above) The storefront is brimming with attractive offers and sections

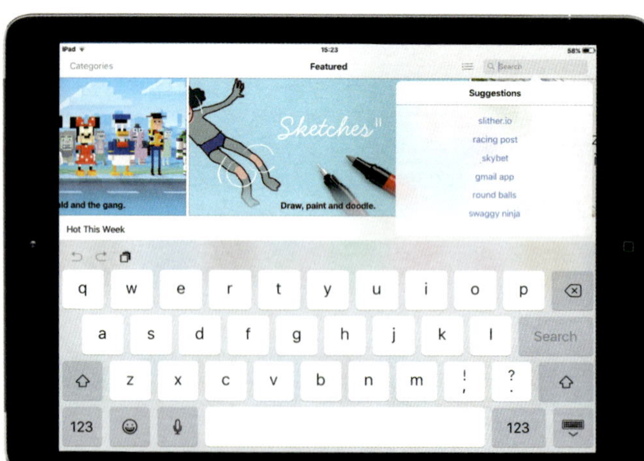

Fig 2 (right) Start typing keywords into the search engine to find what you want

to that page. If you're not sure of what you're looking for, then there are plenty of handy pointers to steer you in the right direction. The 'Featured' section is a good starting point as it showcases all of the latest eye-catching apps of significance. From there you can use the Top Charts and Categories tabs at the bottom of the screen to see what's currently popular or begin searching in an area of interest.

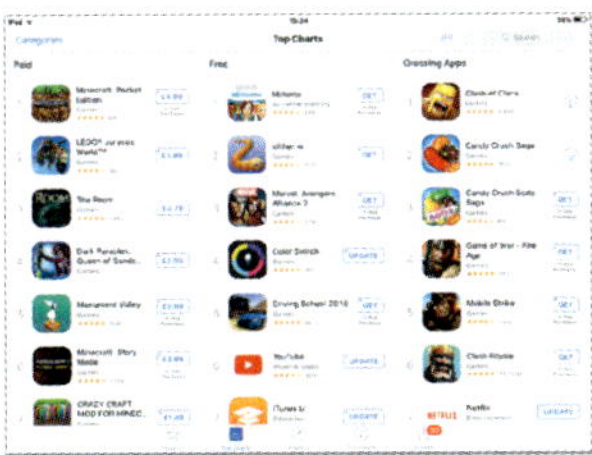

Browse the Top Charts

If you start browsing the App Store without a clue of what to look for or where to go to look for it, then help is at hand. Using the touch icons at the bottom of the screen, tap on the Top Charts section and you will be presented with a rundown of the most popular apps available on the store – both full price and free. You can use this as a barometer to see what's hot in the world of apps and see if any popular apps jump out at you.

Near Me and Wish List

Two features of the App Store introduced back in iOS 7 were the Near Me tab and the Wish List. Near Me tracks your location (you can turn it off by going to Settings>Privacy>Location Services> System Services) and by tapping on the Near Me tab at the bottom of the screen you will be provided with a list of apps that might prove useful based on where you are. Wish List is designed to aid you in your App Store trawling. As you will no doubt come across a wide range of apps that you like the look of and want to buy, but can't necessarily afford them at present, you can add them to your Wish List (tap the share button and choose 'Add to Wish List') which you can access any time by tapping the List icon.

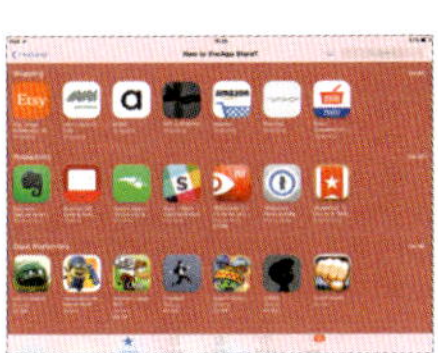

App Collections groups some great apps together for you to browse and download

Update your apps

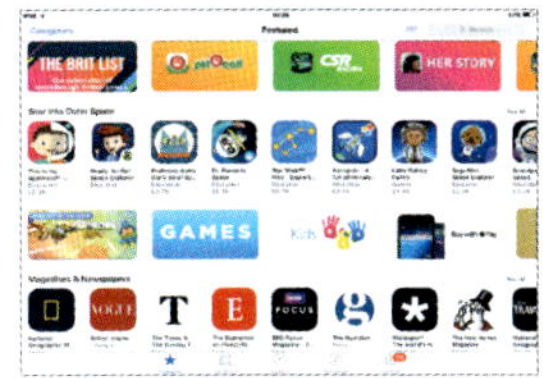

1 Tap on Updates
While in the App Store, tap on the Updates tab at the bottom.

2 Update apps
If an app has an update available, tap on the Update link next to it.

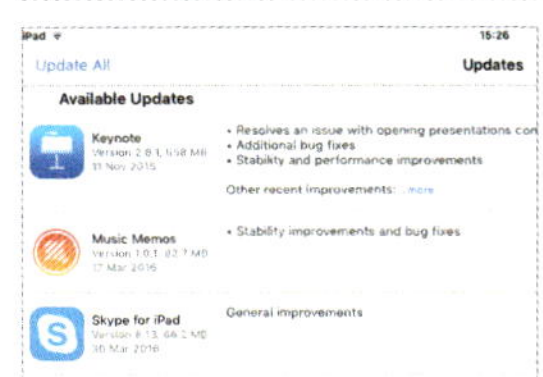

3 Update all
To get all available updates, tap on the 'Update All' link.

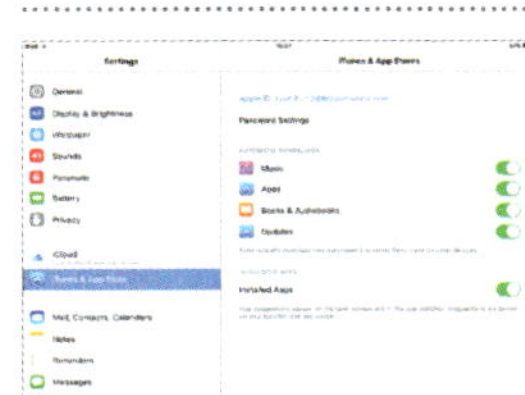

4 Auto update
Go to the iTunes & App Store Settings to set auto-downloads.

App Store

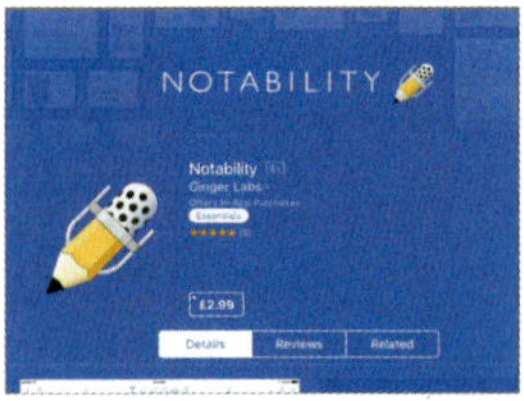

Fig 3 Tap on the price (or 'Free' if it's free) to purchase and download the app. You may have to enter your Apple ID

Purchase an app

Being the only source of gaining apps for your iDevice, the App Store is, as you would expect, a quick and easy way to shop for new apps, and purchasing them really couldn't be simpler. You will already be logged into the App Store with your registered Apple ID, which should have your billing details attached.

If you haven't already added the details of a valid credit or debit card for your app funding then tap on the Featured page at the App Store, scroll down to the bottom and then tap on your Apple ID. Select 'View Apple ID' from the menu and then tap on the Payment Information option. You can now select a card type and enter all of the required information so that all app purchases will be made using that card. Now you can tap on the price of an app and

Featured apps
All the latest significant new additions to the App Store will be showcased in the main shop window under Featured

Buying apps
Tap on the price of a product to initiate the purchase and download process

Store sections
You will be able to access specific stores for Top Charts, Featured, Explore and more by tapping these buttons

Search
Enter keywords into the search field to help you find apps featured within the store

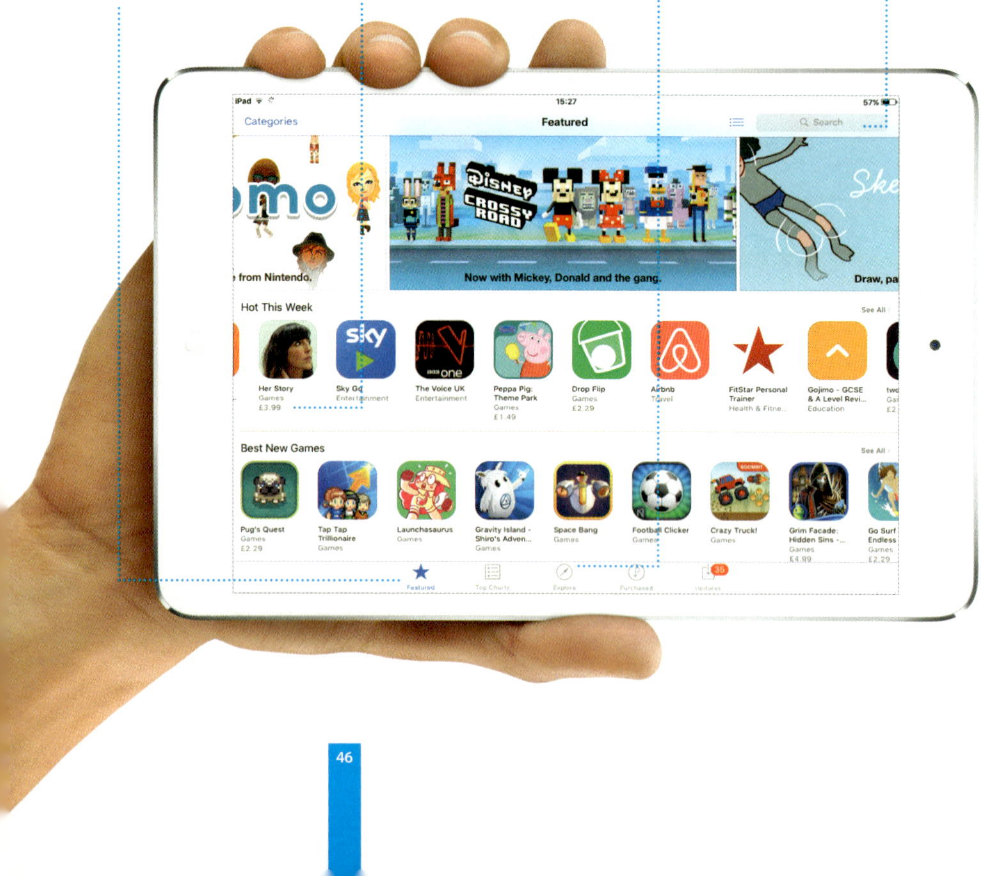

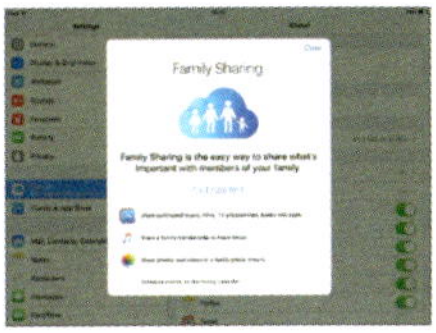

Go to your iCloud Settings to set up Family Sharing to share your purchases with family

then complete the purchase by inputting your Apple ID password (Fig 3). You will still need to enter your Apple ID password when downloading free apps, but you don't have to assign a credit or debit card to do so.

Review and rate apps

App feedback is good, because feedback – good or bad – gets back to the developer and lets them know how the public is receiving their apps and how they can make them better. It also provides information for your fellow iOS users to help them make informed decisions on whether to buy a particular app or not, so if you have the time and the inclination, then why not leave your own mini app review?

To do this, tap on an app to bring up its floating info box and then tap on the Reviews tab followed by 'Write a Review'. Tap on the stars to rate the app out of five – as you tap them they will be coloured in gold. You can add a title and enter your own review text by tapping on the respective field. Once done, hit the 'Send' button to get your review published on the page and info other App Store customers as to the quality of the product.

Submit a review of an app

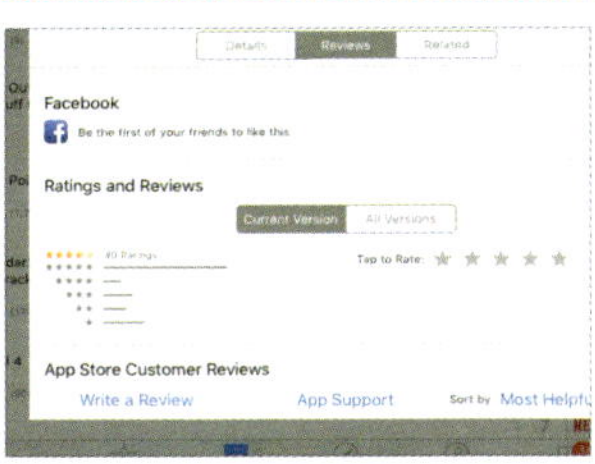

1 Tap to rate
Tap on Reviews and then choose the 'Write a Review' option.

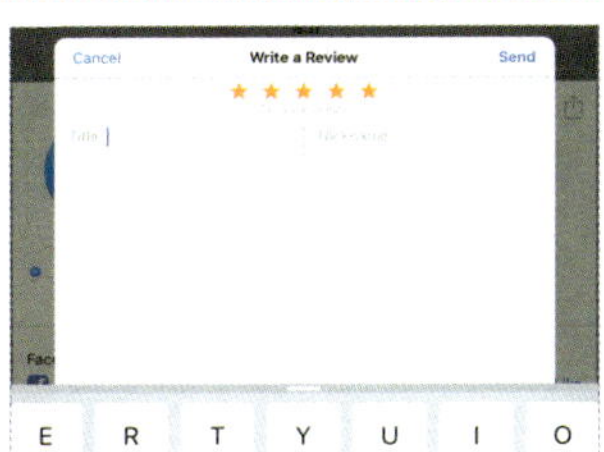

2 Write a review
Tap the stars to rate the app and write a review (you must own the app).

Recommend an app

1 Tap on the Share button
Go to an app's info page and tap the Share button (a box and arrow).

2 Email
If you tap Mail, then you can send an email with the app's info.

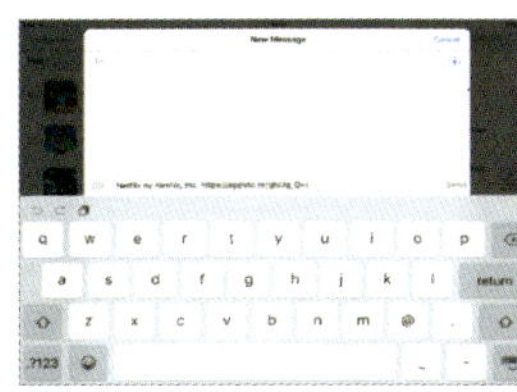

3 Message
Tapping Message enables you to send an iMessage.

4 Tweet
If you have a Twitter account set up, you can also tweet about it.

iTunes

Let your iPad entertain you with music, movies and TV shows – all bought from right here

You'll use it to…

Browse for items
Sections make it easy to find new content and great deals

Purchase media
Buying new music and movies is easy

Discover new media
Search and roam for interesting items

Gift items
Buy and send a gift to a loved one

Make use of Genius
Get artist recommendations and create smart playlists

Get an education
Get access to a wealth of study materials with the iTunes U app

Buy music and movies

Although the new Music app might become your main port of call for downloading music, iTunes still has a lot to offer. You can access the store direct from its own app on the Home screen and browse for content at your leisure. And there is plenty to explore (Fig 1).

The Categories in iTunes

Navigating your way around the iTunes Store is made easy by a series of tabs at the bottom of the screen that allow you to breeze freely to the various store categories that include Music, Films, TV Programmes, Audiobooks and more (Fig 2). Tap on a category to access a front-page relating to that particular category that is packed full of featured offers and attractions.

If you have bought things previously from the iTunes Store on other iOS devices (like an iPod touch) then, thanks to Apple's iCloud service, you will be able to re-download them again onto your iPad

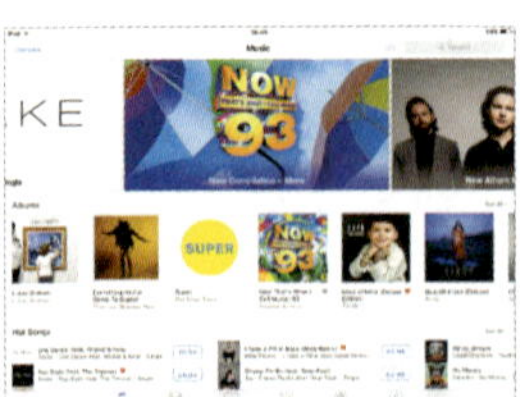

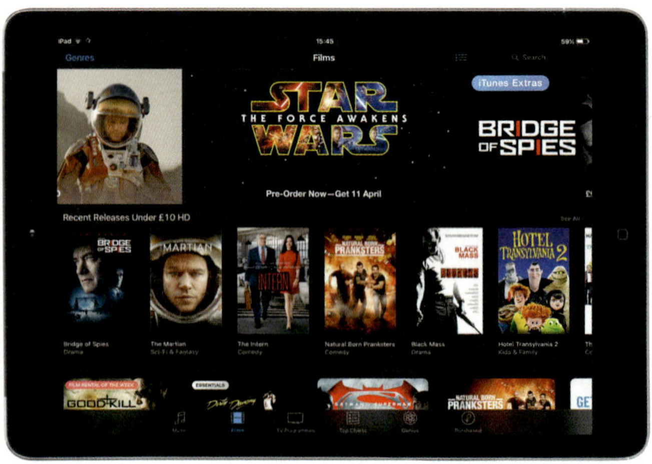

Fig 1 (above) The iTunes Store is a thriving hive of digital entertainment

Fig 2 (right) Use the tabs at the bottom of the interface to jump straight to the various store categories

or iPhone – just tap on the Purchased category, then on the 'Not on this iPad/iPhone' tab at the top of the page and then choose a song and tap on the cloud icon. If you are currently downloading content from the iTunes Store then you will be able to track the progress of your purchases by tapping on the Downloads category.

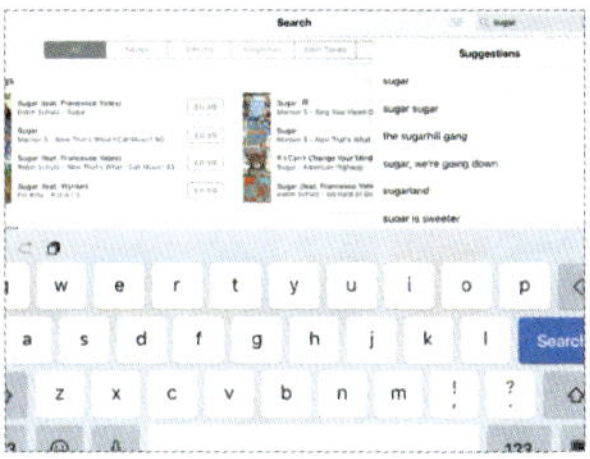

Search for and sample a song

One of the good things about the iTunes Store is that it allows you to try before you buy. First of all, search for an album or artist you may be interested in by tapping the search field in the top corner of the screen. Now tap on an album and then tap on a track name to listen to a sizeable chunk to determine if it is what you're looking for. You can end the preview at any time by either tapping on another song or tapping the Stop button in the middle of the playback wheel.

Download songs

Purchasing and downloading songs from the iTunes Store is a quick and easy process that can be done in seconds. We have already explored how you can search for songs and preview tracks, and if you decide that you would like to go ahead with the purchase then tap on the price and it will turn into a green 'Buy Song' button.

If you then wish to go ahead with the purchase, you will be prompted to enter your Apple ID password before the track will start downloading – this is a security measure to ensure that you don't buy items by tapping on them accidentally. You can track the progress of this by tapping on the Downloads category at the bottom of the screen.

If you are lucky enough to be gifted a redeem code, scroll down the Music page and tap Redeem

Download a TV series

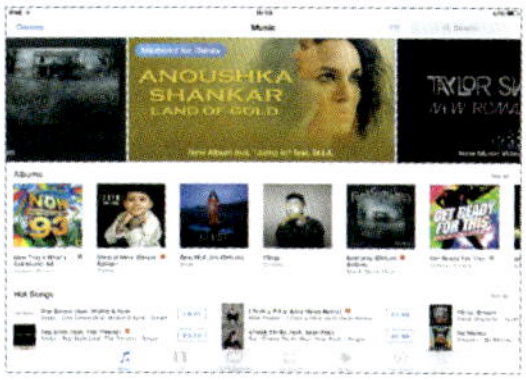

1 iTunes
First, head to the iTunes app to browse the available shows.

2 TV
Tap TV at the bottom and you will be taken to the TV show section.

3 Select a show
Pick a show and it will bring up the information for your selection.

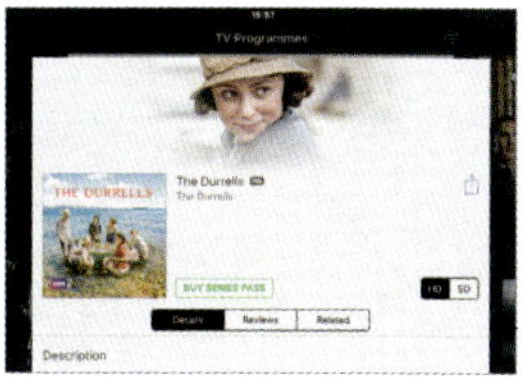

4 Buy the series
Tap the price to buy the series, or check the ratings and reviews first.

iTunes

Fig 3 You can set up Family Sharing by going to your Settings app and tapping on the iCloud settings

Introducing Family Sharing

Family Sharing is a feature that came as part of the iOS 9 update and it presents a new way to bring harmony to your family's digital life. Up to six people can share purchases from iTunes, iBooks and the App Store without sharing accounts and you can also pay for your family's purchases from one credit card and approve what your children buy from the parent's device. You can set up Family Sharing in your Settings app. Just select the iCloud section and you will see the option to 'Set Up Family Sharing' (Fig 3).

iTunes Match

Since iTunes works in perfect harmony with Apple's iCloud service, any music that you purchase, regardless of which device you're

Store sections
You will be able to access specific stores for Music, Films, TV Programmes, Audiobooks and more at the bottom of the screen

Featured sections
All of the latest significant new additions to the iTunes Store will be showcased in the main shop window and heavily flagged

Buying
Tap on a product to start the purchase and download process. Ensure you are logged in and have funding set up

Search the store
Enter keywords into the search field to find specific artists, songs, movies or programmes featured within the store

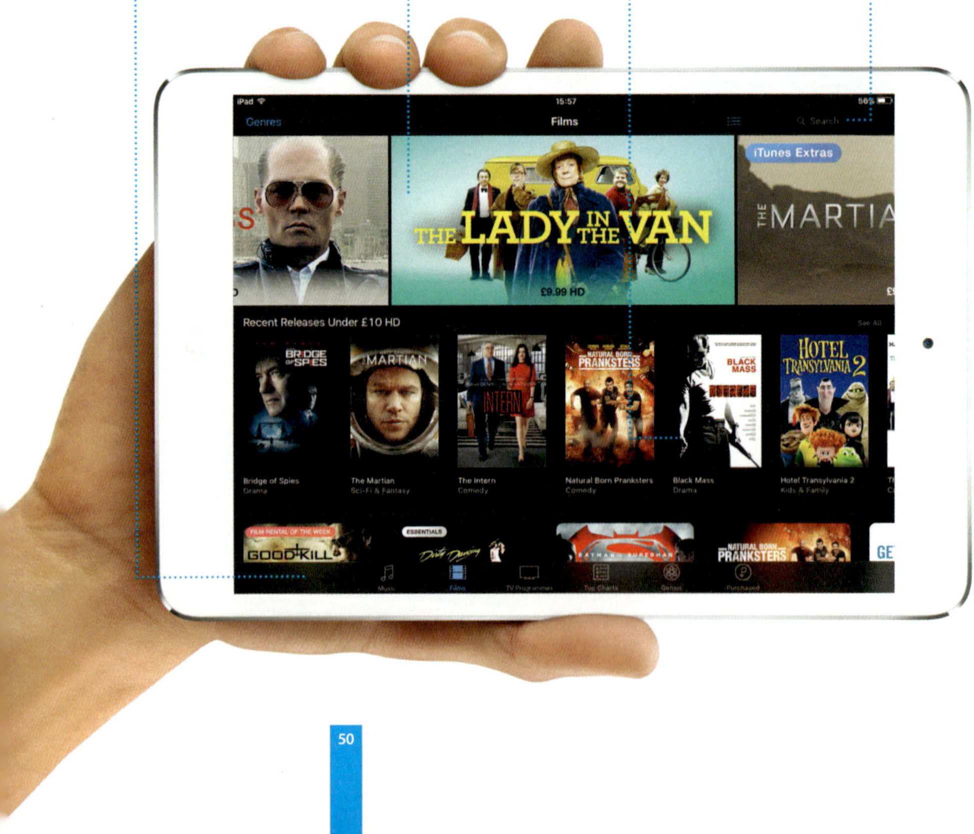

Re-download past purchases by tapping the Purchased tab followed by 'Not on This iPad'

using to make the purchase, will be automatically pushed to your other iOS devices. iTunes Match (which requires an annual subscription) is an extension of this service which matches the music on your computer, that has been imported from CDs, to its digital iTunes Store counterpart, and stores it all in your iCloud ready for use. iTunes determines which songs in your collection are available in the iTunes Store and any music with a match is automatically added to iCloud for you to listen to at any time, on any device. Since there are more than 20 million songs in the iTunes Store, chances are your music is already in iCloud.

iTunes in the Cloud

With iCloud, the music that you purchase in iTunes appears automatically on all of your mobile iOS devices and Macs running OS X Mountain Lion or above. Any music you have purchased in the past will also be easily accessible. Simply tap on the 'Purchased' tab and you will be able to view an alphabetical list of all of your past purchases. If one of the items isn't currently on your device then highlight it and then tap on the cloud icon that is next to the song name. The song will instantly start downloading to your device.

Buy a ringtone

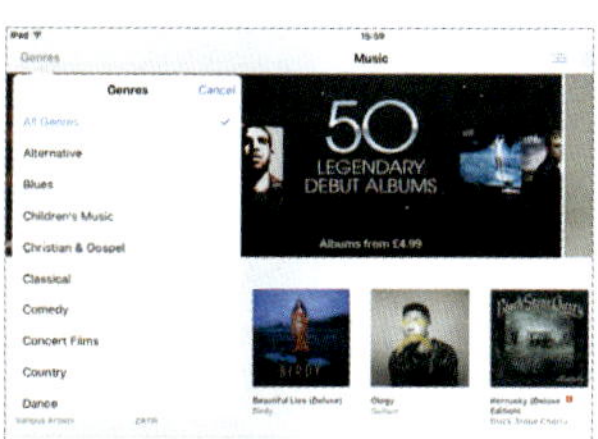

1 Tap Genres
Tap on the 'Genres' option in the top-left corner and choose 'Tones'.

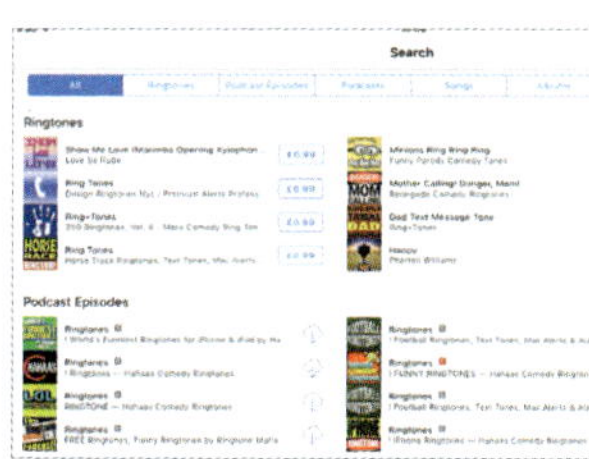

2 Select the style
Tap on a style to jump to the section and browse what is available.

Add to Wish List

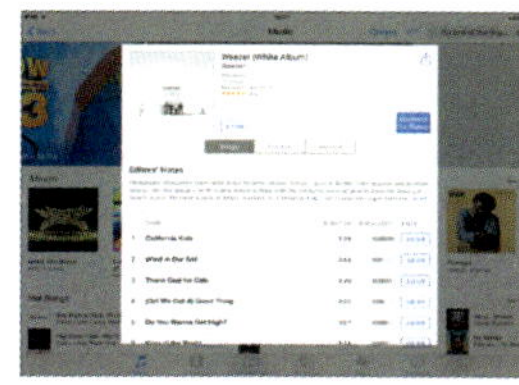

1 Find a product
When you like the look of a product, tap on the share icon.

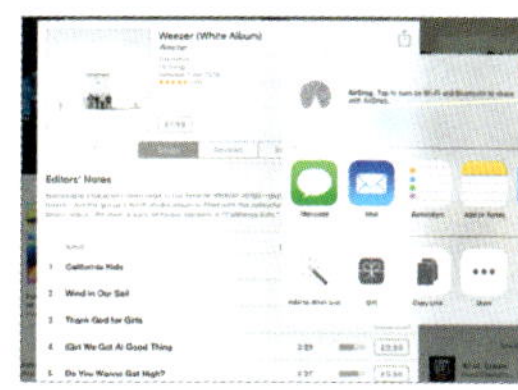

2 Add to Wish List
Select the 'Add to Wish List' option from the pop-up window.

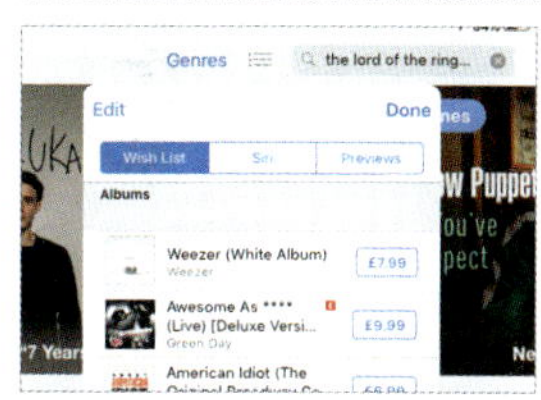

3 View list
To see your Wish List, tap the list icon next to the Search field.

4 Previews and more
See songs you have sampled by tapping the 'Previews' tab.

Music

The Music app enables you to stream music through Apple's own music streaming service

You'll use it to...

Play music
Belt out your tunes with the Music app's simple set of controls

Make playlists
Create new playlists on the fly quickly and easily

Stream music
Subscribe and stream unlimited tracks through the Apple Music service

Connect
Follow and connect with the bands and artists who matter most to you

Hear radio stations
None-stop music of any genre piped straight to your device

Search content
Find what you want when you want to listen to it

Listen to music on the go

Originally introduced to prominently push the new Apple Music streaming service, Music is also where you can listen to all of the top tunes that you have synced or purchased on your device and create new playlists to suit any occasion (Fig 1).

Import songs

There are numerous ways to import music to play on your device. The most direct route is by purchasing it straight from the iTunes Store on your device, and you can do this by launching the iTunes app, browsing the Store and tapping on the prices to download the tracks or albums to your device. While in the iTunes app, you can also tap on the Purchased tab at the bottom of the interface and this will list all of the music that you have bought previously on other devices (by tapping the 'Not on This...' tab).

Thanks to the power of iCloud, all of your previous purchases are tracked, so tap the cloud icon to re-download it on your current device. Of course, you can also import songs by connecting

Fig 1 (above) All of the music purchased through the iTunes app can be played in Music and you can create playlists

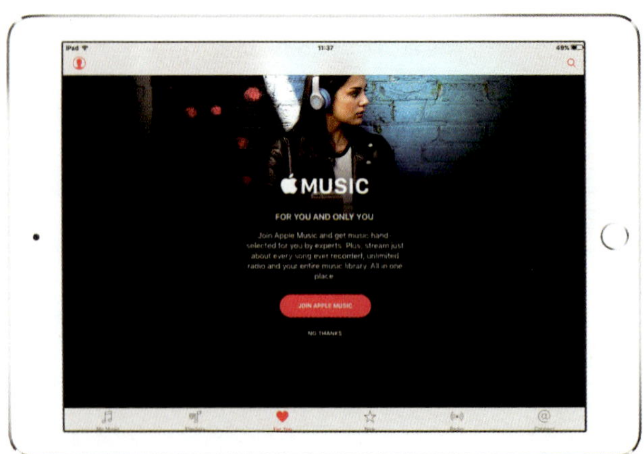

Fig 2 (right) The new Apple Music service lets you stream unlimited music through your device, allowing you to savour more

your device to your computer and syncing through iTunes or, alternatively, opening iTunes on your computer, highlighting songs in your music library and then manually dragging them to your connected device in the left-hand column.

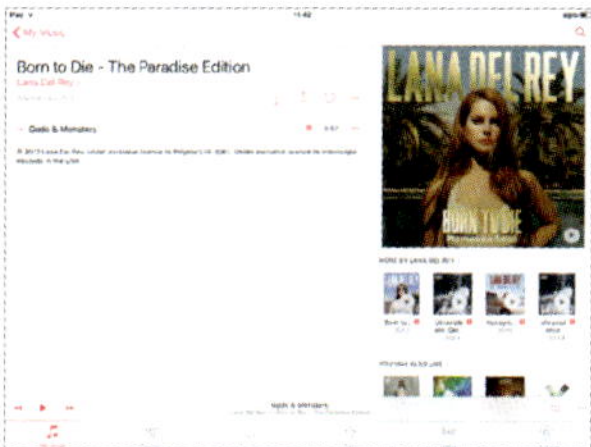

Play your music

First and foremost, the Music app is there to enable you to play and listen to music on your device, and the controls for doing this are simple to get to grips with. Start off by choosing music to listen to by selecting the 'My Music' tab at the bottom of the screen and navigating to a song, then tap on it to start playing it. The controls at the bottom of the interface allow you to play/pause the current song and skip to the next or previous songs.

Experience Apple Music

The new Apple Music service has been pushed to the forefront of the Music app, and for good reason. Set to rival Spotify's music streaming service, Apple Music requires a monthly subscription fee (although you can try it free for three months) but for that you can stream unlimited music through your device, allowing you to savour the very latest releases from your favourite artists, when you demand them, without having to buy the albums (Fig 2).

Tap on the 'For You' tab at the bottom of the screen and you will be treated to a tailored selection of music from Apple Music based on the type of tunes that are in your personal collection. You can also tap on the 'New' tab to discover all of the latest releases. It's a great way to keep up with the current music trends and experience a wider range of music through your device.

Go to the Music section in Settings to adjust the EQ and volume limits, amongst other things

How to unsubscribe to Apple Music

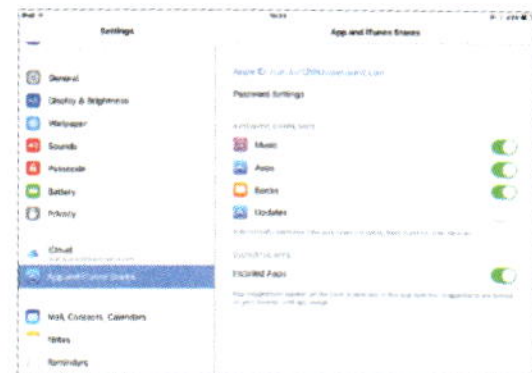

1 Launch Settings
Launch the Settings app and then tap on 'App and iTunes Stores'.

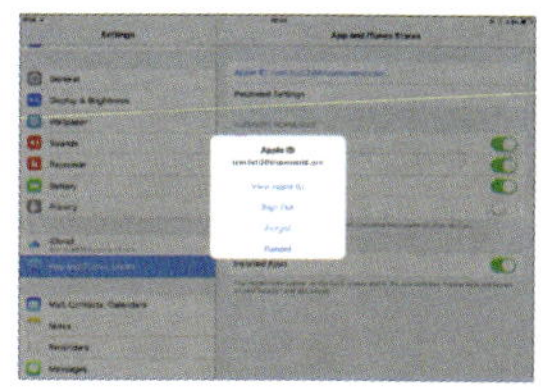

2 Go to Account Info
Tap on the Apple ID option at the top and choose 'View Apple ID'.

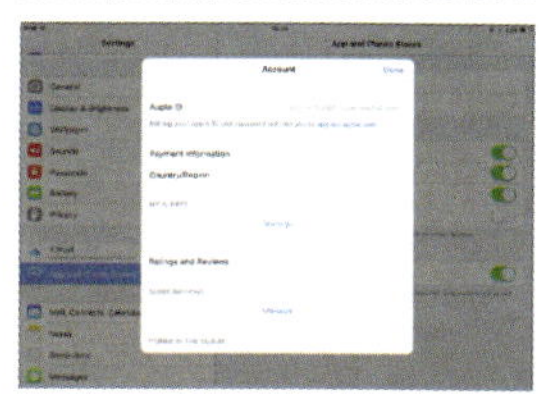

3 Manage subscriptions
Sign in and then tap on 'Manage' in the Subscriptions section.

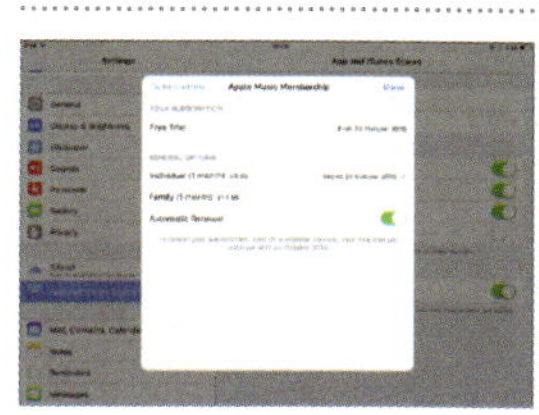

4 Your Membership
Tap on 'Your Membership' and then turn off 'Automatic Renewal'.

Fig 3 Listen to your favourite genres of music, minus the monotonous DJs, through the Radio section…

Your personal radio stations

Another great aspect of Apple Music is the Radio feature. Tap on the 'Radio' tab at the bottom of the interface and you will be able to browse stations dedicated to any type of music that you enjoy listening to.

Here you will find featured stations or, by scrolling further down the screen, be able to pick the genres of music that appeal to you. Once done, the selected station will instantly start playing, providing great music without you really having to lift a finger. More importantly, you don't have to suffer tiresome DJs talaklikingn go over tracks and generally loving the sound of their own voices! All of the stations that you listen to will be stored under the 'Recently

Repeat and shuffle
At the bottom of the screen you will notice controls to Repeat this track and to turn on Shuffle

Like
Tap the heart icon to 'like' a song. The Music app will then base future recommendations on the songs that you like

Volume control
You can pump up the volume by dragging this slider to the right position. Press and hold and move the slider

Playback controls
You can play/pause and skip songs using the simple set of controls at the bottom of the screen

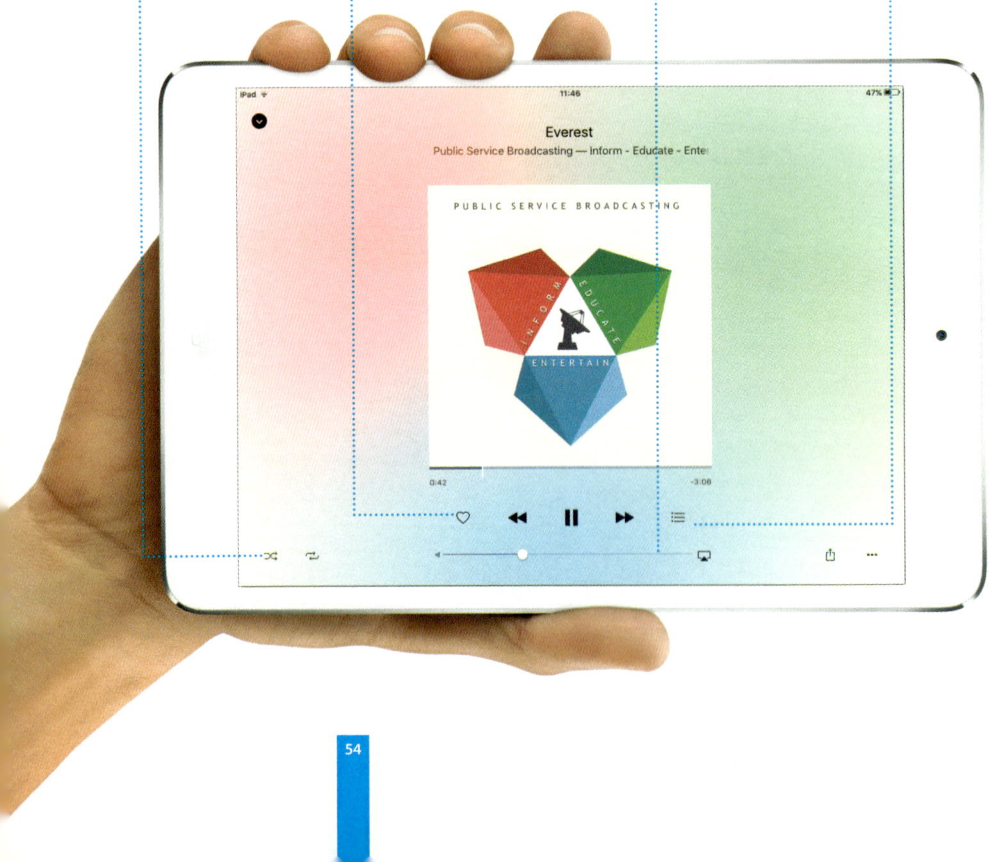

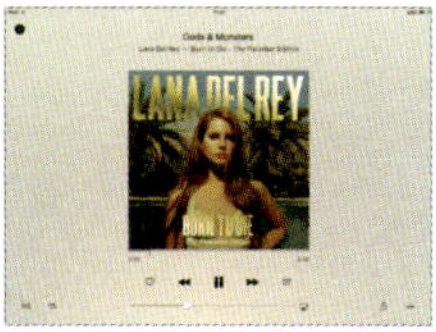

You can scrub through songs by pressing on the line under the artwork and then dragging it

Played' setion at the top of the Radio tab, so you can jump in and start listening to them again quickly and easily (Fig 3).

Another cool aspect of Apple Music is the 'Connect' category. This allows you to connect with your favourite bands and artists and follow their latest tweets and updates in one handy digest, without having to trawl through your, no doubt, heavily-populated Twitter feeds to find the information that you want.

Create and manage playlists

Creating and managing playlists on your device is easy through the Music app. As well as creating new playlists from scratch, you can also edit playlists that have been synced across from iTunes in order to update them or make subtle tweaks here and there.

To create a new playlist, simply tap on the Playlists tab and then tap the New button in the top-right corner. Give your new playlist a name, tap Save and then start adding songs from your library by either tapping on the song itself or the '+' icon next to it. When you have finished adding, tap Done and your playlist will be complete. If you wish to edit an existing playlist, select it from the Playlists page and then tap the Edit button.

Create a playlist

1 Tap on New
On the Playlists screen, tap New, name your playlist and then tap Save.

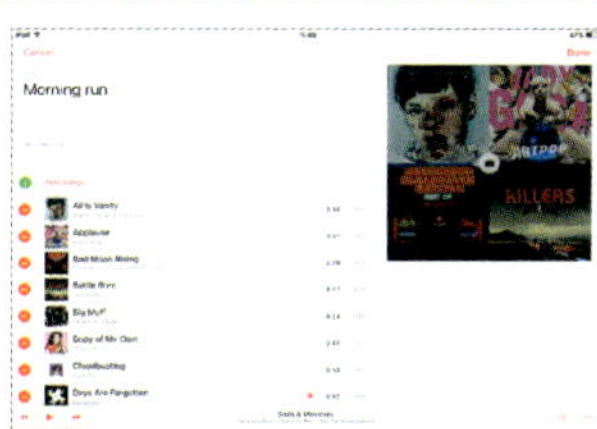

2 Add songs
Add songs by tapping on a song name or the '+' icon.

Connect to artists

1 Tap on Connect
Select the 'Connect' tab and then 'Find more Artists and Curators'.

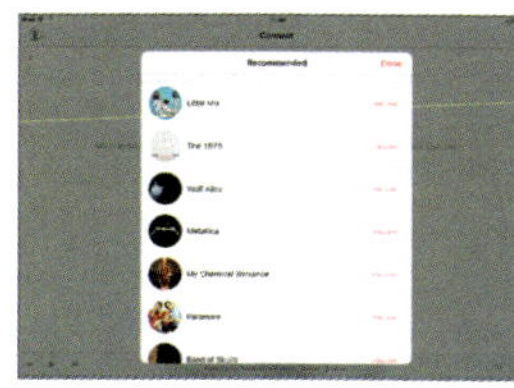

2 Select artists
Scroll down through the list and tap 'Follow' next to an artist.

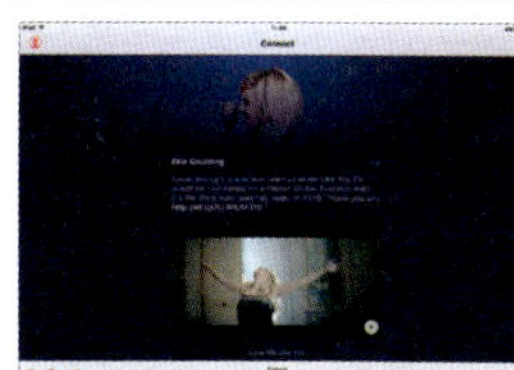

3 Scroll artists
Scroll down the page to see updates from your faves.

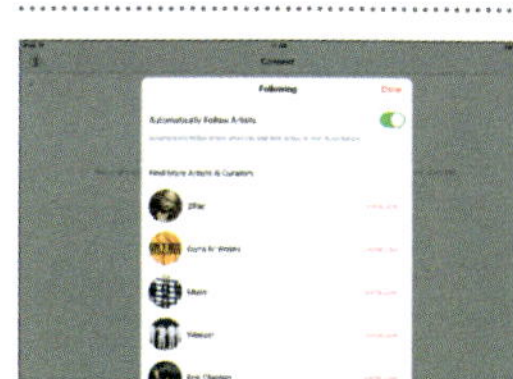

4 Edit whom you follow
Tap 'See who you are following' and then tap 'Unfollow'.

Videos

The Videos app lets you watch movies and TV shows anywhere on your iPad

You'll use it to...

Watch videos
Watch films, music videos and TV shows on your iPad

Shop for content
Access the iTunes Store in-app to shop for videos

Stream to Apple TV
Beam your videos straight to the big screen

Stream videos from your computer
Watch your computer video library remotely on your iPad

Watch anywhere
Take your device with you and watch videos wherever you are

Manage your movies
Sync files from your computer and delete them once watched

Fig 1 (above) Viewing movies and TV shows on your device is simple through the Videos app

Watch TV shows and movies on iPad

You can use your iPad to watch movies, music videos and TV shows, transforming it into a mobile multiplex to view what you want, on demand. Using the Videos app is easy, so sit back, relax and enjoy the show (Fig 1).

Rent and buy from iTunes

Just like the Music app, Videos features a launch pad to the iTunes Store, in this case the visual entertainment section – where you can shop for films to rent or films to buy outright. Simply tap the Store button in the top-left corner of the main Videos interface to be warped to the iTunes Store and then use the search field to find what you want.

When you have found a film, tap on the View button next to the title and a box will appear that provides a plot synopsis, credits, details and user reviews (Fig 2). More importantly it also features a

Fig 2 (right) Tap a movie in iTunes and then choose to buy or rent it. Note that both options aren't always available

button that allows you to preview the movie through your Videos app and options to buy or rent the movie. If you're buying then the system is the same as purchasing music or apps – just tap 'Buy' and the film will download to your device.

Renting is slightly different – you still download it, but it will expire after a certain number of days and, once you start a movie, you have a limited amount of time to finish watching it. It does mean you will never have to pay a late fee though!

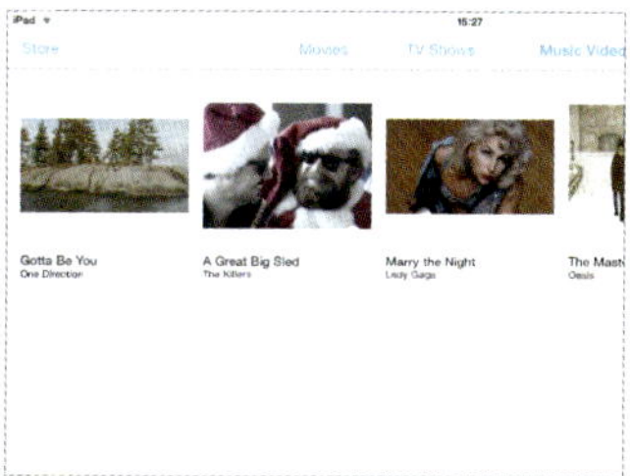

Import videos from your computer

If you don't want to buy directly from the iTunes Store through the app then you can also import videos from your computer via iTunes. Simply connect your device and then click on the Movies section under your Library to view all of the movies on your machine. Now you can either drag the film to your iDevice, which is in the sidebar, or perform a sync instead to get your flicks onto your device.

Playing your videos

Playing videos on your device is easy. From the main Videos app screen, use the tabs to choose to view Movies, TV Shows or Music Videos (located at the top on the iPad, at the bottom on the iPhone) and then tap on a video that is displayed in your chosen section.

When the video is launched, a simple set of controls at the bottom of the screen allow you to play or pause the action, skip chapters and adjust the volume. You can also scrub through the action by swiping along the bar at the top of the screen and go full-screen by tapping the button in the top-right corner.

You can also adjust the viewing area size by double-tapping anywhere on the screen

Change scrub speed

1 Tap scrub bar
Press your finger down on the dot situated on the scrub bar.

2 Scrub rate
The scrub rate will be displayed (either high or half-speed).

3 Swipe down
Slide your finger down to change to the alternate speed.

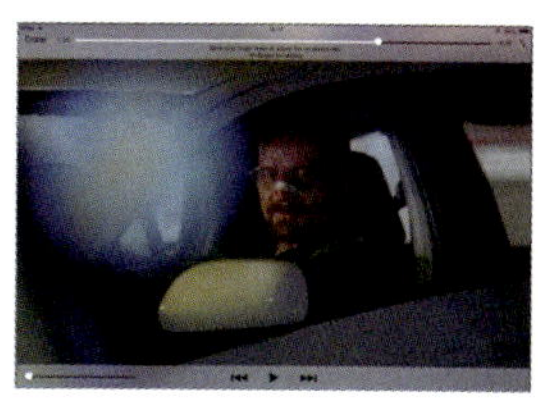

4 Start scrubbing
You can now slide your finger along the bar at the selected rate.

Videos

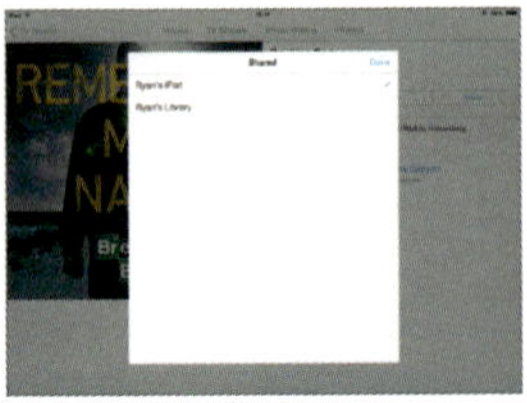

Fig 3 You can access your Mac's movie library to watch on your iDevice

Home Sharing

With Home Sharing, you can play movies and TV shows on your iDevice from the iTunes library on your Mac or PC. To use this feature, both your iDevice and your computer need to be on the same Wi-Fi network and, on your computer, you must have iTunes open and running. In iTunes, click on the Advanced menu and then turn on Home Sharing and ensure that both your computer and iDevice are logged in and using the same Apple ID.

To ensure that you are logged into the same Apple ID on your iDevice, go to Settings, tap on the Music or Videos sections and then log your details under the Home Sharing section. Once the

End viewing
If you wish to stop watching, tap the Done button and resume where you left off later

Playback controls
Simple controls let you play and pause the action, skip backwards or forwards through chapters and adjust the volume

Rewind
Press and hold the dot on this bar, and by sliding it to the left you can rewind the action

Screen size
Tapping this button will make the video fill the screen. Tap it again to return to the original dimensions

With iPad 2 or later, you can mirror the screen on a TV wirelessly using AirPlay Mirroring and Apple TV

system has been set up, a new tab will appear at the top of your Videos interface called Shared. Tap on this and then choose to access your computer's library (Fig 3). Now simply select something to watch, sit back and enjoy. To deactivate this service, click on the Advanced menu on your computer again and then turn off Home Sharing to instantly sever the connection.

AirPlay

If you have an Apple TV system in your home then you can stream video content from your device to your TV wirelessly using AirPlay. This is easy to set up and means that you can use your iPad or iPhone to shop for movies to buy or rent and then use your device as a remote control to play them on your big TV screen.

To start streaming video with AirPlay, start playing a video on your iDevice and then tap the AirPlay button. Next, choose your Apple TV from the list of AirPlay devices and then select it to start beaming the video across. If the AirPlay button doesn't appear or your Apple TV doesn't appear in the list, check that both devices are connected to the same wireless network. You can also stream videos using various cables, including AV cables and VGA Adapters. Your device will also connect to Apple TV through AirPlay in the Control Centre.

Streaming videos with AirPlay

1 Via Control Centre
Bring up Control Centre, tap AirPlay and select an option from the menu.

2 Via the app
You can also select to project via AirPlay from within the app.

Delete videos

1 Locate video
Find a video that you no longer want on your device.

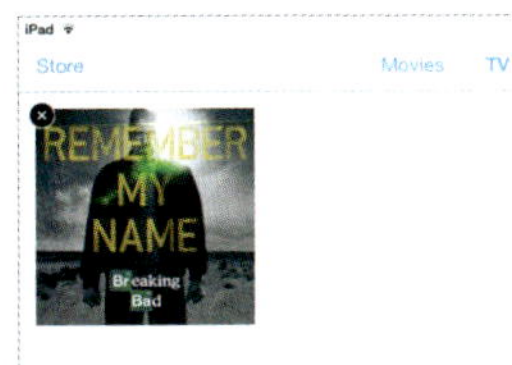

2 Press and hold
Tap the Edit button and an 'X' appears in the corner.

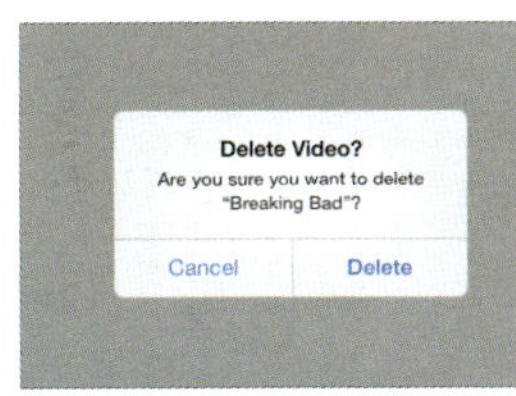

3 Tap to delete
Tap on the 'X' icon and a message will appear asking if you're sure.

4 Instant removal
Tap Delete and the video will be deleted (you can redownload it).

Safari

Safari is the main platform for browsing the web on your iOS device; we showcase how to use it

You'll use it to…

Browse the internet
Use Safari to search or view websites on your iOS device

Open tabs
Browse for new content in new tabs while leaving the original web page running

Save for offline reading
Web pages in Safari can be saved later for offline reading

Private browsing
Enable Private browsing to keep your browsing history private

View Shared Links
View links shared by people you follow, for example on Twitter

Save favourite pages
Use bookmarks to save all your favourite websites

Surf with ease

Safari has benefited a great deal from updates in iOS 8 and 9, such as the addition of intuitive multi-touch gesture controls for manipulating web content and Keychain/iCloud integration to allow your saved passwords and credit card details to be stored and accessible across multiple devices. You even have a universal search/URL bar at the top which provides quick access to websites or words within a page. Ever since the iOS 8 update, you can be browsing a page on your iPhone and then pick up your iPad to see the same page displayed without you having to lift a finger.

Browse the web

Launching Safari for the first time will usually open with a blank canvas. But in future use it will present you with either your saved bookmarks (which we cover later) or the last page you visited. Tap on the universal search/address bar at the top to enter either a

Fig 1 (above) Safari benefits from quick search/URL access, enhanced iCloud integration and multi-touch controls

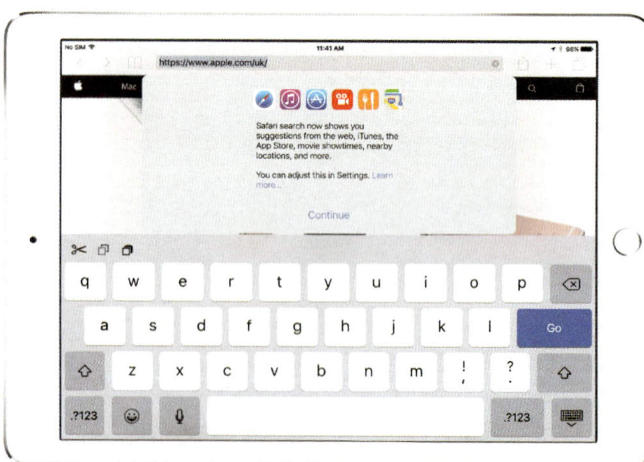

Fig 2 (right) The new search/URL address bar at the top provides many functions to help you browse the web

dedicated URL address eg **www.google.co.uk** or you can type in a search term, eg Xbox One. While typing your search/address you will notice it start to automatically display results. This allows you to quickly access the page without typing it out in full. Additionally the search bar can be used to search for words within pages. For example, if you re-tap the search bar and type in Games and then scroll down you will see the option 'On this page'. Once this is selected a series of arrows will appear at the base of the screen and these can be used to zip through all the words.

Finally, navigating content is much easier by the ability for you to swipe forwards and backwards between pages you have read. Simply long press on the left or right edge of the screen and drag the page across.

Browse with tabs

While browsing there may be times when you want to continue viewing your current page, but at the same time need to access additional websites or search results. Instead of closing the current page down and using forward/back controls to switch between pages you can use the tabs system instead. Click on the top '+' icon (or the new page/'+' icon for the iPhone) to launch a new tab. You can now type in your URL or search term and then switch back to your other tabbed page by simply clicking on it (or once again for iPhone users, the new page icon will display the previous tabs).

If you like browsing the web on multiple devices (iPhone, iPad, Mac) then iCloud tabs also come in handy to allow you to access all of your open tabs on one device on your other devices. Tap on the tabs button and a list of the sites open on your other devices will be accessible from the bottom of the screen.

Safari Reader

Most modern websites, unless they have a responsive design, will not be completely formatted to take advantage of your iOS device's screen size (iPhone more so). Or if they are, the content may be riddled with ads, comments, links or other pop-ups getting in the way of your reading experience. To help, the Safari app has a

Go private

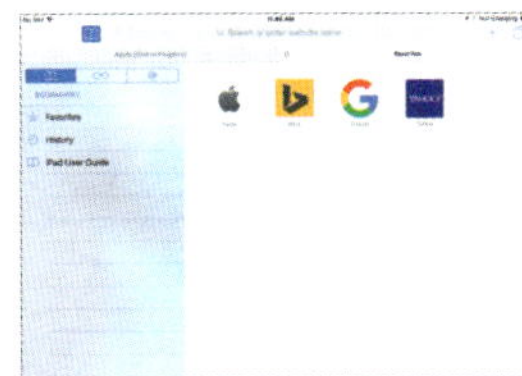

1 Tap tabs
For private web browsing, start off by tapping the tabs button.

2 Tap Private
Tap on the 'Private' option in the top-right corner of the screen.

3 Access the tab
In private mode any tabs you create won't be remembered.

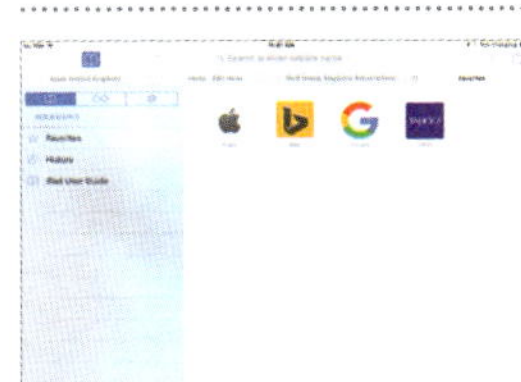

4 Cover your tracks
To end the private session, close all tabs and tap 'Private' again.

Safari

Fig 3 (above) The Safari Reader function is useful for viewing content without the distractions associated with websites

function which allows you to enable a dedicated reading mode: Safari Reader. This option is subtly placed inside the search/URL bar (towards the far left side) and it looks like a series of horizontal lines. By simply tapping this icon the text and embedded images on a web page will transform and display down the page in a scrollable list. This makes reading the content much easier and more straightforward. Additionally, you can tap on the 'a/A' icons at the top of the screen to increase or decrease the size of the text to allow for easier reading.

Offline Reading List

Browsing the web on Safari is pretty easy to do, but the key ingredient to its continued functionality is the requirement of an internet connection. Unless you have a dedicated data contract

Cloud icon
If you have enabled iCloud support you can use the cloud icon to access tabbed pages from other iOS devices

Search bar
The universal search and URL bar at the top provide quick access to web content

Bookmarks
Any bookmarks you save are accessed via the Bookmark icon or listed under the URL bar for iPad users

Tabbing
You can quickly add new tabs to the browser in order to keep the original page intact

To share a website, tap the share icon to the right of the address/search bar and pick a service

enabled on your iOS device you will rely on an available Wi-Fi connection to get the required internet access. Even if you tether your iPad to another to get your browsing fix on the fly this is still scuppered if the source signal strength is poor.

Thankfully, Safari has a built-in solution for this already and it's called Reading List. This option will allow you to quickly save a currently viewed web page for reading later on in an offline environment when there is no internet connection available. Simply tap the share button and then choose 'Add to Reading List' to save new pages.

Bookmarks bar

Adding bookmarks is a process that allows you to save your favourite webpages for fast retrieval when you need them later on. It's handy to use for websites you check frequently. Saving bookmarks simply involves selecting the Share icon to the left of the search/URL bar and then choosing Bookmark. Once saved, your chosen bookmarks will be accessible via the Bookmark icon displayed underneath the bar. Alternatively if you tap the search/URL bar you can view them in a handy thumbnail view.

Add a page to Reading List

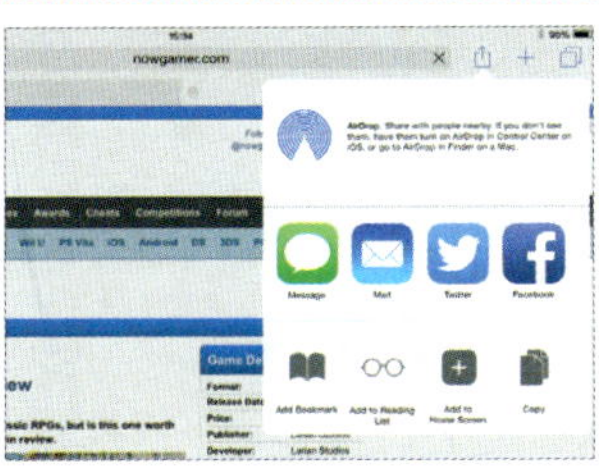

1 Add page
Tap the Share icon next to the search bar and select Add to Reading List.

2 Access Reading List
Tap the bookmark and then the glasses icon to access the page.

Add Home screen links

1 Access your website
First you will need to browse to a website.

2 Share icon
Now tap the Share icon and choose Add to Home Screen.

3 Name your shortcut
Tap the name field to rename the bookmark.

4 Add to Home
Click on Add and the icon link will appear on your Home screen.

Mail

With Apple's versatile Mail app you can send emails and receive every message from every account into one handy inbox

You'll use it to...

Link accounts
You can activate the Mail app with any valid email address and password

Send and receive
Keep up to date with email arrivals and quickly send out new messages

Manage accounts
Add as many accounts as you like

Organise your messages
Store and save messages safely away

Find emails easily
Mark certain people as VIPs to access their emails from a special mailbox

Get emails quickly
No need to press anything, just get your emails downloaded automatically

Manage your email

Your iPad's built-in Mail app is brilliant for sending and receiving emails, so you don't have to carry a laptop everywhere with you to keep in touch. You can also get all of your different email accounts linked to the app so every email from every account is streamed into one handy inbox and you'll never have to worry about missing an important one again (Fig 1).

Link an account

If you are using the Mail app for the first time then you will need to set up and tether an account to the app. This is a quick and easy process that requires no more than a valid and active email address and an account password (Fig 2). Once set up, select your account in the 'Inboxes' section of the Mailbox column and then all new messages will instantly be downloaded for that account.

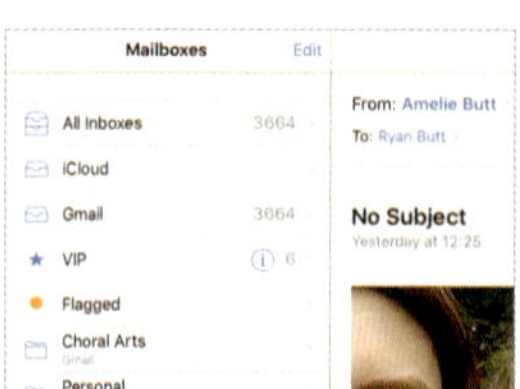

Fig 1 (above) Every one of your email accounts, together at last

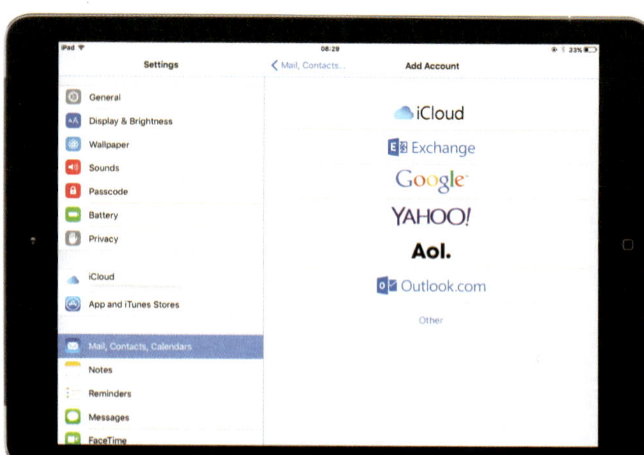

Fig 2 (right) Once you have set up an account, go to the Settings app to link more accounts to your Mail app

You can determine when all new emails are pushed from the servers to your mailbox by launching your Settings app, tapping on the Mail, Contacts, Calendars section and then selecting the Fetch New Data option. Activate the Push function and determine exactly when the messages will be received. To ensure that you get all new mail as soon as possible, tick the 'Manually' option to get all new mail pushed straight to your device as and when. Your device will also now automatically scan for new mail when you launch the app.

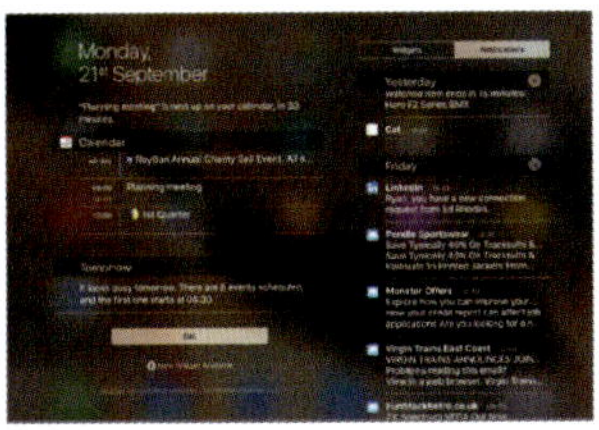

Mail and Notifications

One of the many good things about the Mail app is that you don't have to manually press a button to download new messages from the server, it just happens automatically whenever you open the app. What's more, if you have the Mail app listed in your Notification Centre then you will get alerts on your screen whenever a new email is received. You should also ensure that Mail is activated in iCloud Settings so that all of your messages – received and read – are synced to all of your devices.

Write and send an email

Writing and sending emails is easy through the intuitive Mail app interface. To compose and send an email, simply tap on the pen and paper icon in the top-right corner of the Mail interface and a blank email will appear. Fill in the recipient's email address, enter a subject and some body text and then hit the 'Send' button.

You can also mail out attachments, such as photos and documents from within the other respective apps by tapping on the sharing icon (which is represented by a small rectangle icon with an arrow in it).

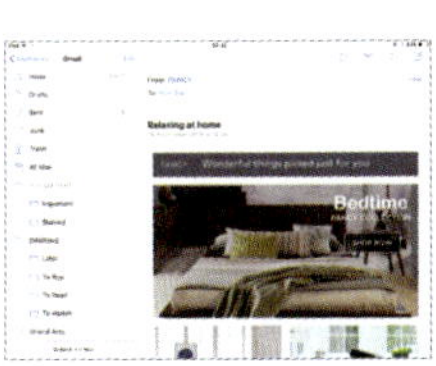

You can move emails to different mailboxes by tapping the file icon at the top of the interface

Search for an email

1 Tap Search
Tap on the Search field (top of the inbox on iPhone, top-left on iPad).

2 Enter text
Use the keyboard to type in some keywords to search for.

3 Results
Emails containing matches will be listed. Check to find the right one.

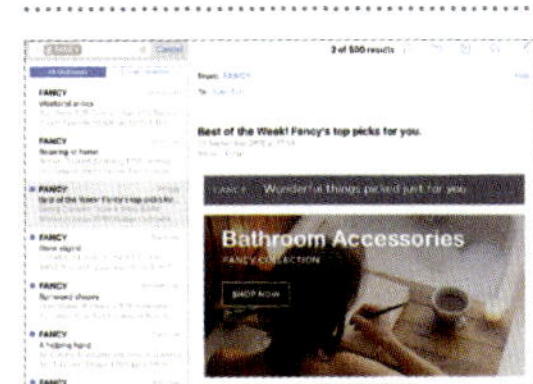

4 Return to normal
Tap the Cancel button to return your mailbox to normal.

Fig 3 Go to Mail, Contacts, Calendars in Settings and then tap 'Add Account' to include a new mailbox

Manage multiple accounts

It's very rare these days that folk just have one email address. At the very least, most would have a work and a personal account. The Mail app is versatile enough to incorporate virtually any type of email account within a few easy steps and, handily, you can stream all of your mail from all of your accounts into one main inbox, making it easy to track all aspects of your life simultaneously. To add a new account, launch your Settings app and then go to the Mail, Contacts, Calendars section.

Under the Accounts section at the top of the page you'll see the option to 'Add Account' (Fig 3). Tap this and then choose the type of account you will be adding – these include Gmail, Yahoo!, AOL, Hotmail and more. Once you have selected the account, enter a name, email address and password for that account and, after a few seconds of verification, the account will be added to your

VIP
You can add certain senders to a VIP mailbox, to keep high-importance emails separate

Inbox
Tap here to see all your received emails. If you have multiple accounts then this option will say 'All Inboxes' instead

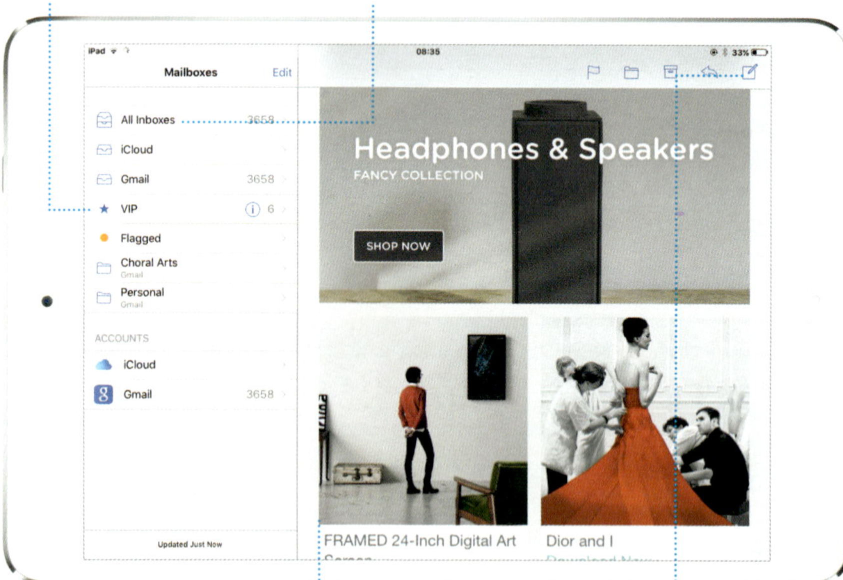

Your emails
When you tap on an email it will be displayed in the main window, whereby you can archive, delete or reply to it

Composing emails
Tap on this icon to start composing a new email. Your address will show up in accordance with the account you are using

> To remove people from your VIP list, tap on the sender and then choose 'Remove from VIP'

active inboxes within the Mail app. Within Mail, you can tap on an individual mailbox to view only the emails relevant to that account, or you can tap on All Inboxes to view all of your received emails in one handy stream.

VIP mailboxes

With each new iOS release, Apple is continuously redesigning Mail with a more streamlined interface for easier searching, reading and writing. One of the recent new features is VIP Mailboxes. You can set up a VIP list so that you'll never miss an important email – whether it's from your boss, your best friend or your accountant. To mark a person as a VIP, all you have to do it tap on their email address in a received message and then, on the Sender screen, select the 'Add to VIP' option. A star will then appear next to that person's email address to confirm that they have been marked as a VIP. This star will also be present next to all emails received from that person in your inbox. You can also find VIP emails quickly thanks to your new VIP inbox – just tap on this mailbox and all of the emails from your VIPs will be stored there for easy reference – you'll never have to search your entire inbox for important messages again.

Mark a person as a VIP

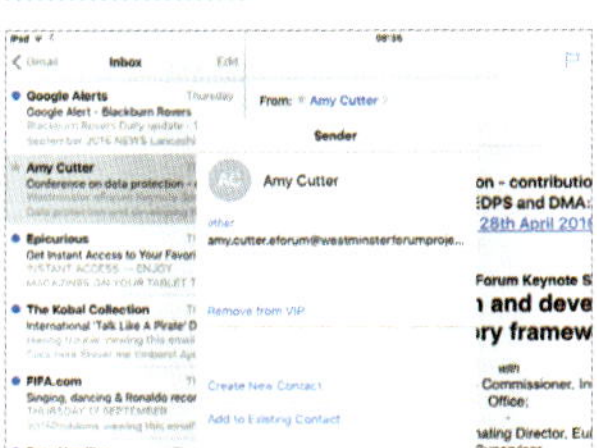

1 Highlight sender
From your inbox, open an email and then tap on the sender.

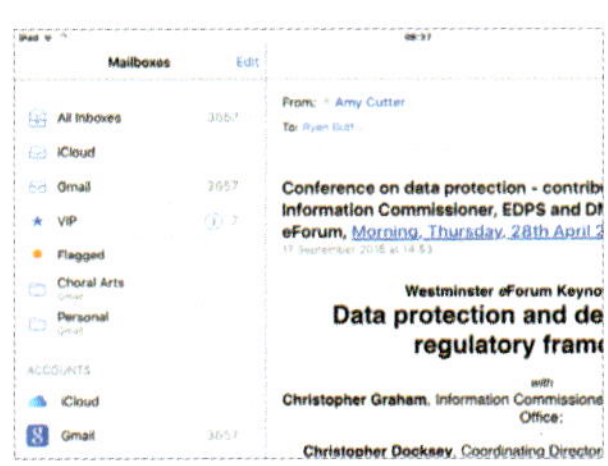

2 Place a star
Tap 'Add to VIP' and all emails from that person will go to your VIP inbox.

Mark or flag messages on your device

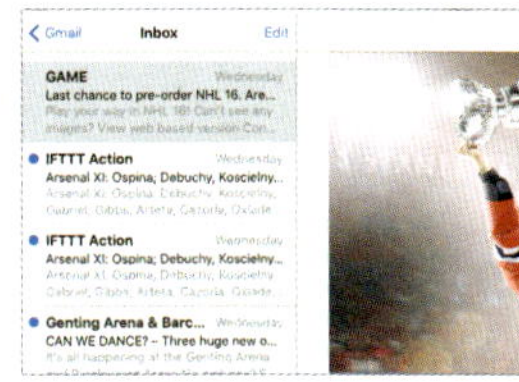

1 Go to inbox
While in a mailbox, highlight a message in the list to the left.

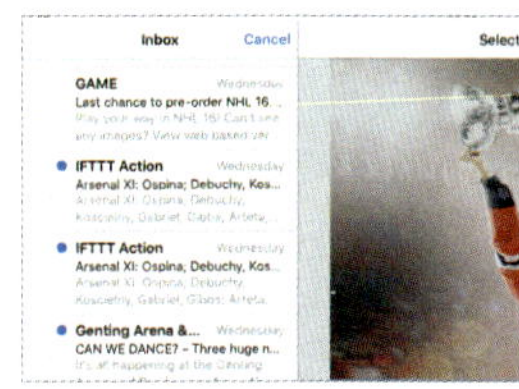

2 Tap Edit
Tap the Edit button in the top-left corner of the column.

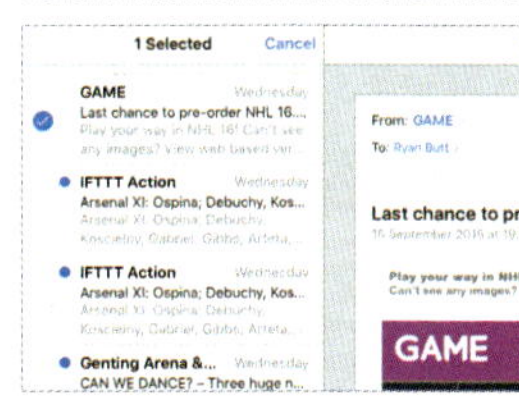

3 Tap to tick
Place a tick next to the message and then tap Mark.

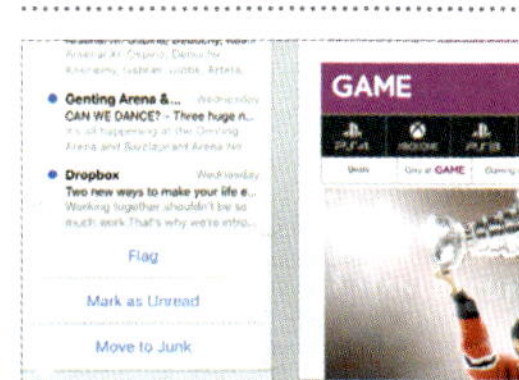

4 Choose option
You can now choose to Flag or Mark as Read.

Calendar

You'll never miss an important event again with the iPad's built-in date-keeper

You'll use it to...

Schedule events
Create new events for yourself and others

Plan ahead
View calendars by day, week, month or year

Sync with other devices
Get key dates from your other desktop calendars imported

Manage calendars
Activate or disable individual calendars

Get alerts
Set reminders for key events

Add birthdays
Import birthdays and anniversaries from your Contacts app

Keep up to date in Calendar

Your iPad's Calendar app is an intuitive way to keep up to date with events for the day, week, month or indeed the next 50+ years, and scheduling event dates into the app is as easy as selecting a calendar view and tapping on the '+' icon (Fig 1).

Schedule appointments

Making appointments is a quick and easy process in the Calendar app. Use the tabs at the top of the interface to select the Day view and you will see the current day broken down into hourly time segments. To choose a future day, tap on the day in the monthly calendar to the left and a breakdown of the day will be presented on the left-hand side of the interface. You can swipe up or down to scroll through the selected day, and then to start scheduling an appointment, press and hold on the desired time segment. A New Event banner will then appear on the time segment, quickly followed by an Add Event box (Fig 2). Here you can enter a title and

Fig 1 (above) With the Calendar app you can schedule events and appointments far into the future

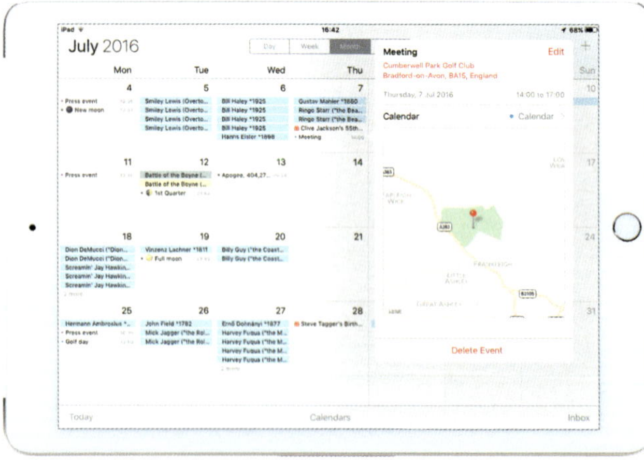

Fig 2 (right) Press and hold on a time segment to bring up a box that lets you add numerous details to your event

location for your appointment or event and then factor in the start and end times. Using the other options in this box, you can then choose to repeat the event, invite people from your contacts (and, thanks to the latest iOS update, check their availability), trigger alert reminders, add it to a particular calendar and add notes.

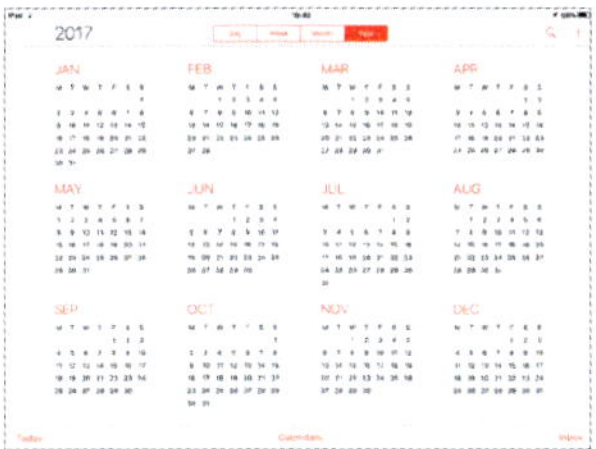

Changeable views

When you launch the app you will see a variety of views, accessible by tabs at the top of the interface. By default the view is set to Day, with the current day broken down into one-hour segments, but you can easily tap another tab to view the calendar by Week, Month, Year or List. In Month view you don't see the timing of each scheduled event, but you can easily spot your busiest days. The List view displays your daily calendar with a list of all commitments for the month to the left of it.

Multiple calendars

One of the best things about the Calendar app is its versatility in allowing you to create different calendars for different areas of your life, which you can then merge into one main calendar or deactivate at will via the Calendars menu. It is even possible to sync your Facebook events with your calendar so you don't miss out.

You can also create new calendars in the desktop Calendar app on your Mac (by clicking the File menu and choosing New Calendar). Any new calendars that you create can then be synced to your iPad Calendar app via iCloud. This should happen automatically but you can speed up the process by tapping the sync button at the top of the Calendars menu.

You can also start scheduling new events by tapping the '+' button in the top-right corner

Create an event

1 Find the date
Use the view tabs to find the date you wish to schedule on.

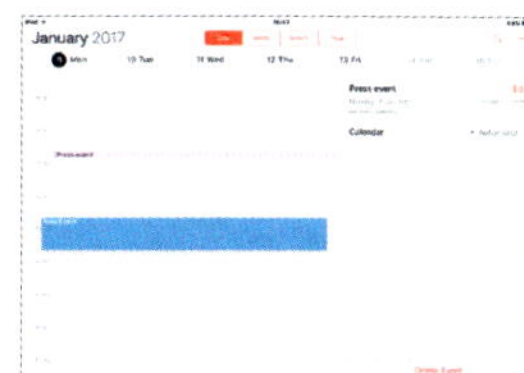

2 Scroll to time
Swipe up or down through the Day view. Tap on the start time.

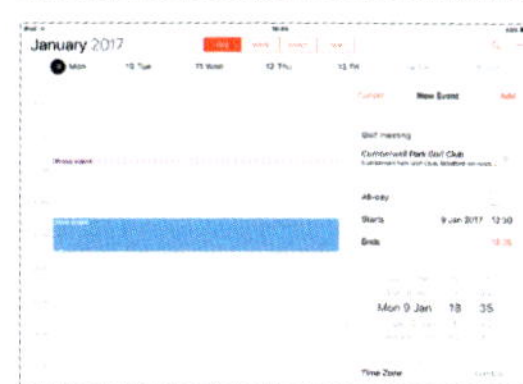

3 Press and hold
Add details into the Add Event box that appears.

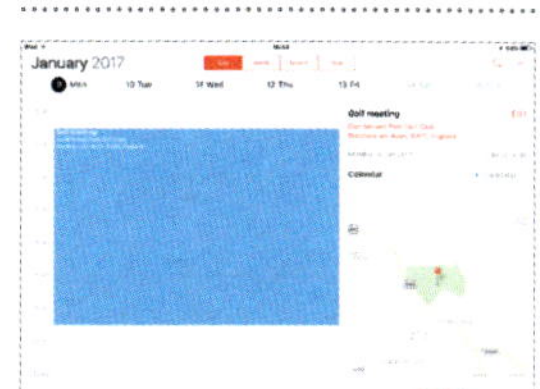

4 Enter details
Enter locations and start and end times and then hit Add.

Fig 3 Tap on the Calendars button and ensure that the Birthdays calendar is activated in the list

Sync birthdays and anniversaries

As you would expect from a built-in iOS app, Calendar works in perfect unison with other apps to make your life easier. In this instance, Calendar works with your Contacts app to display birthdays and anniversary dates that you have assigned to specific people within your Contacts database.

Ensure that you have birthdays assigned to people in your Contacts database and then, in your Calendar app, tap on the Calendars button at the bottom of the interface. Scroll down to the Other section, where you will see Birthdays and then ensure that this option is selected (Fig 3). All birthdays and anniversaries assigned in your Contacts app will now be displayed as all-day events on the corresponding day in your calendar. To assign birthdays and anniversaries to specific people on Contacts, tap on

Calendar views
The row of tabs at the top of the interface will allow you to view calendars by Day, Week, Month, Year and List. Tap on a tab to change the view

New events
To create a new event, click the '+' symbol in the top-right corner of the interface

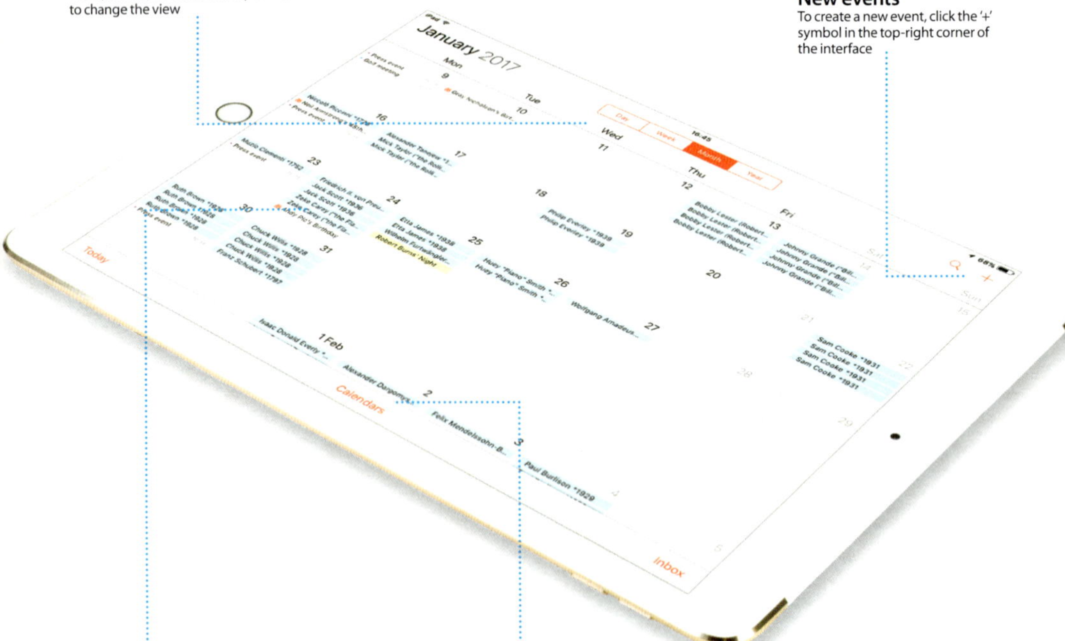

Events
A breakdown of the day shows all scheduled events. Tap on an event to view or edit the details

Your calendars
Tap on the Calendars button to view all active calendars and those you subscribe to. You can manage calendars from here

You can also add events to a Calendar by importing a Calendar (.ics) file from an email

a contact and then choose Edit. Scroll down to Add Field and tap '+', then scroll down and choose to add either a Birthday or Date before factoring in the dates concerned.

Manage multiple calendars

Through the Calendar app you can subscribe to any calendar that uses the iCalendar (.ics) format. Many calendar-based services support calendar subscriptions, including iCloud, Yahoo! and Google – it's just a case of hunting around for the right ones.

To subscribe to a calendar, go to your Settings app and then choose the 'Mail, Contacts, Calendars' option. Under Accounts, tap Add Account and then choose Other. From here you can select the Add Subscribed Calendar option.

You can also subscribe to iCal or other .ics calendars published on the web. As we have mentioned, you can also create new calendars in your Mac's desktop Calendar app and then sync them to your iPad via iCloud. To manage your calendars, tap the Calendars button at the bottom of the interface and a list will display all available calendars that you can then enable or disable at will.

Subscribe to new calendars online

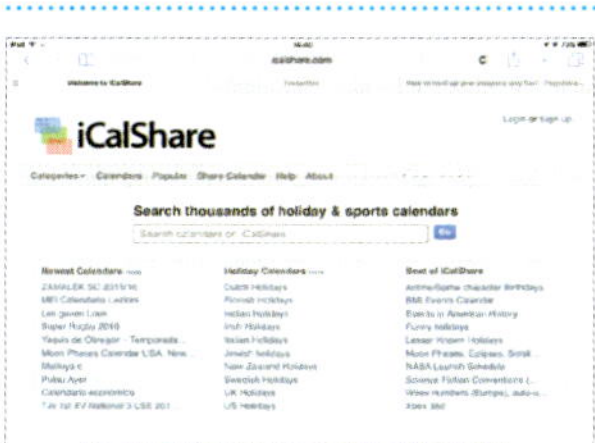

1 Find calendar
Search for iCal calendars online and then hit the Subscribe button.

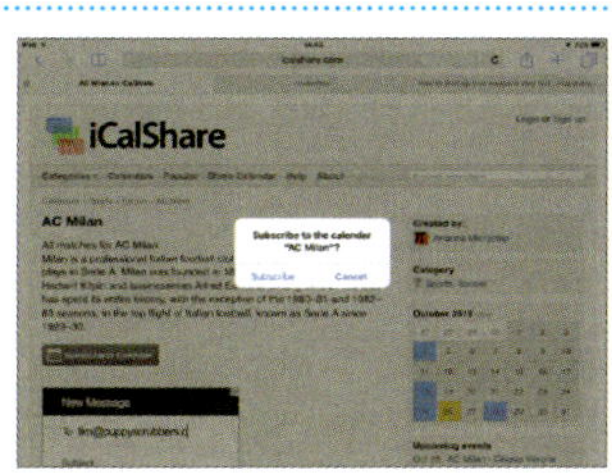

2 Activate new calendar
The calendar will be added and can then be activated from the list.

Set event alerts

1 Tap on event
Tap on an existing event or create a new one by pressing '+'.

2 Tap on Alert
Tap Edit, then scroll down and then tap on the Alert option.

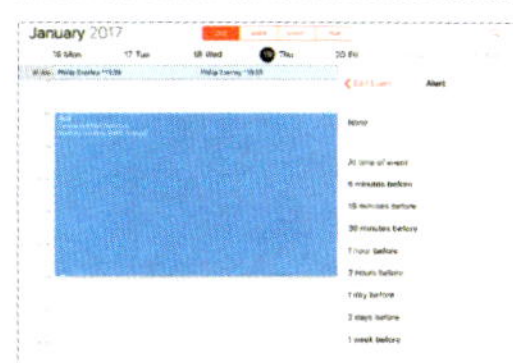

3 Select a time
From the list, select an option for when you want to be alerted.

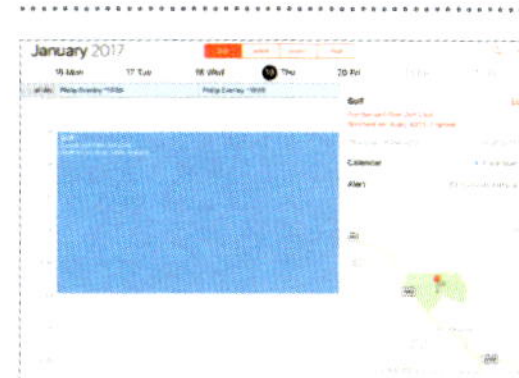

4 Tap Add
Now tap on Done and then your iPad will automatically alert you.

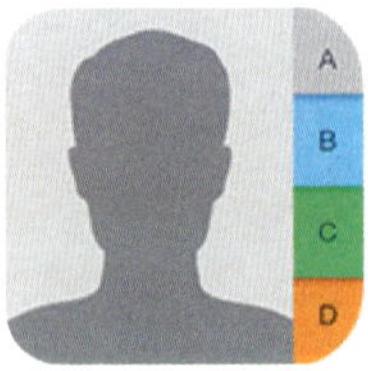

Contacts

With the Contacts app, you can access and edit your contact lists from personal, business and organisational accounts

You'll use it to...

Access Contacts
Maintain personal and business details

Edit Contacts
Add and delete details

Search Contacts
Access your contacts quickly

Address emails quickly
Open an email from the Contacts section

Sync contacts
Transfer Contacts to multiple devices

Assign photos
Attach a photo to a contact for visual recognition of a person

Manage your contacts

Contacts allow you to not only access your friends and associates but you can edit them from a selection of personal and business accounts. You can also search for details within thanks to an easy search field and send emails by clicking on an address (Fig 1).

Add, edit and delete Contacts

To add a contact on the iPad or iPhone you need to tap the Contacts app, which will open the Contacts window. This displays a list of contacts, in alphabetical order, on the left-hand side of the screen with the intimate details of each contact displayed on the right-hand side of the screen.

To Edit your contact database and add a new contact, tap the '+' button situated in the centre at the bottom of the screen. A new screen will open up displaying an empty template which you can fill in via the pop-up keyboard present at the base of the screen

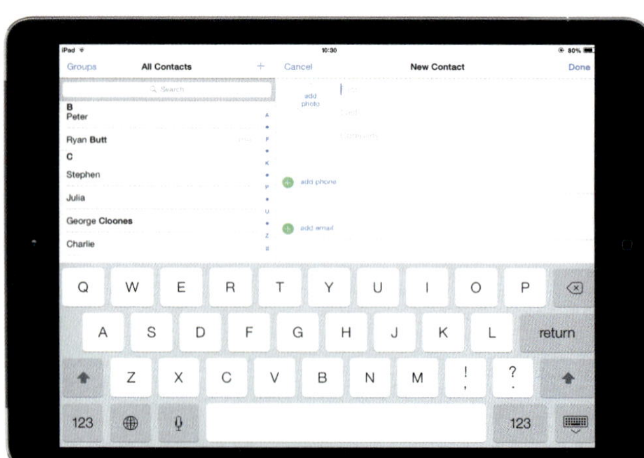

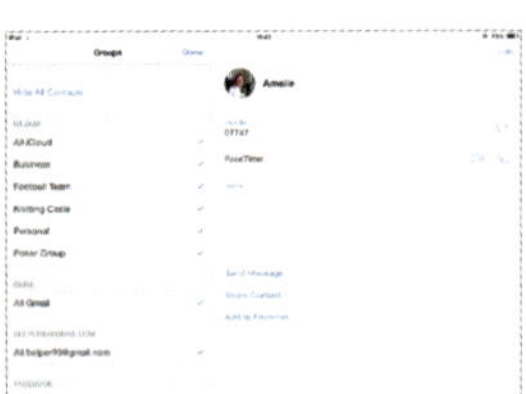

Fig 1 (above) You can use the Contacts information within other apps, adding efficiency and convenience

Fig 2 (right) To enter data on each template line, touch the line and enter data via the iPad's floating keyboard

(Fig 2). When you have completed the page, press Done to close the record and return to the index. To edit an existing record, press the Edit button situated in the centre at the bottom of the screen. This time, the completed template will be present with options to either change the text or delete entire lines of information using the swivelling red buttons that turn into delete buttons when touched.

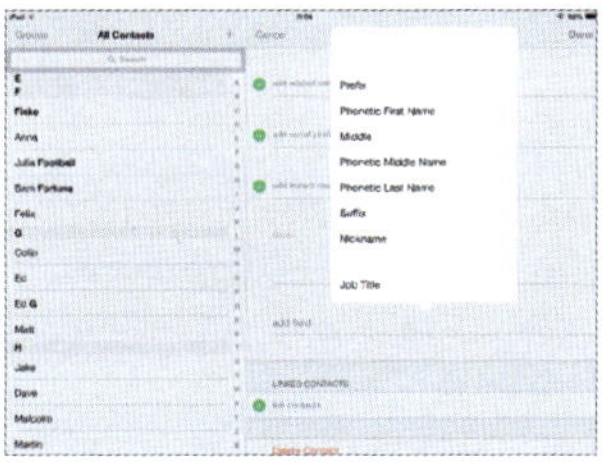

Add extra information to your contacts

When you access the edit screen for a contact, you are presented with a standard template array that asks you basic information. You can, however, add further information if you wish which is not readily observable from the basic edit page. To see it, you have to press the '+' key, which will bring a pop-up box displaying a wide choice of extra fields, including Twitter information, nickname, Instant Message information, birthday and related people.

Contacts & iCloud

Keep your contact details, including your mail contacts, up-to-date across all your devices (including a MacBook or other laptop, iMac or PC, iPhone or iPad) with the iCloud storage facility.

Contacts are stored in your iCloud account and pushed wirelessly to your other iOS devices and computers that are set up with the same iCloud account. To make sure that the iCloud and Contacts are working together, go to the Settings app on your iPad and tap the iCloud section on the left-hand side of the screen. On the right-hand side of the screen, swipe the button next to the Contacts header to On.

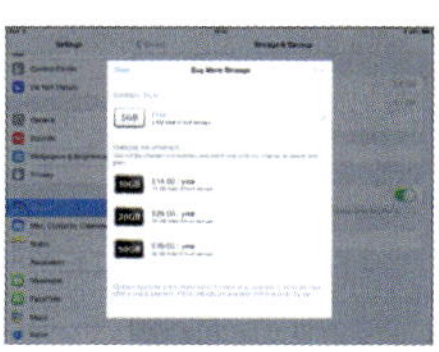

If your iCloud storage is insufficient to store your Contact information, you can purchase more

Assign a photo to a particular contact

1 Edit mode
Enter the Contacts app and tap on a new or current contact.

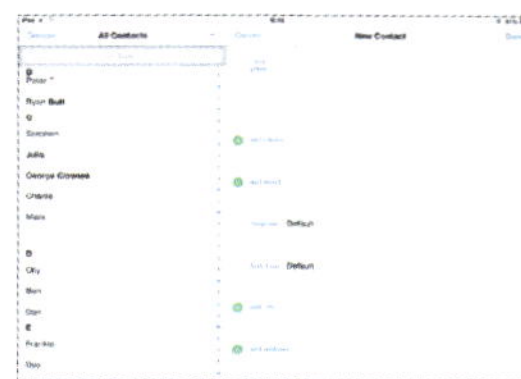

2 Add a photo
If it is not visible, scroll to the Add Photo box and tap on it.

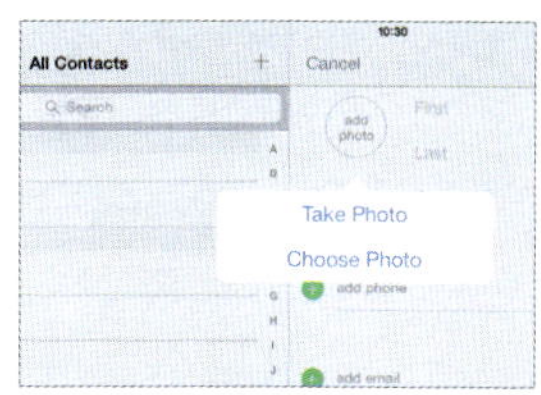

3 Take or choose
Via the menu, choose to either Take Photo or Choose Photo.

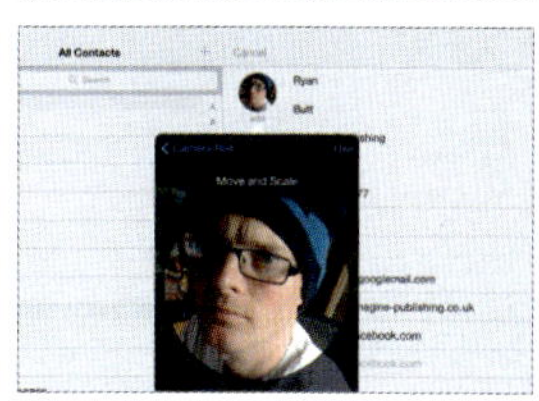

4 Insert photo
Use your device to take a photo or import from your photo archive.

Contacts

Fig 3 Tapping on a contact's address will open the Maps app and take you to that particular location

Integrate with other apps

It is possible to integrate the Contacts apps with other apps to form a seamless connection and also to allow you to perform tasks without having to pause to copy and paste from one app to another, or pause while one program is stopped and another opened. A good example is the Maps app.

If you open a current contact which features a full address, just tap on the address and this action will automatically open the Maps app (Fig 3). The Maps screen will then be displayed and that app will attempt to provide a visual indication of the address itself, giving you information on the location but also providing you with the opportunity to set up directions from your current location to that address. Similarly, if you list a website within the Contacts app,

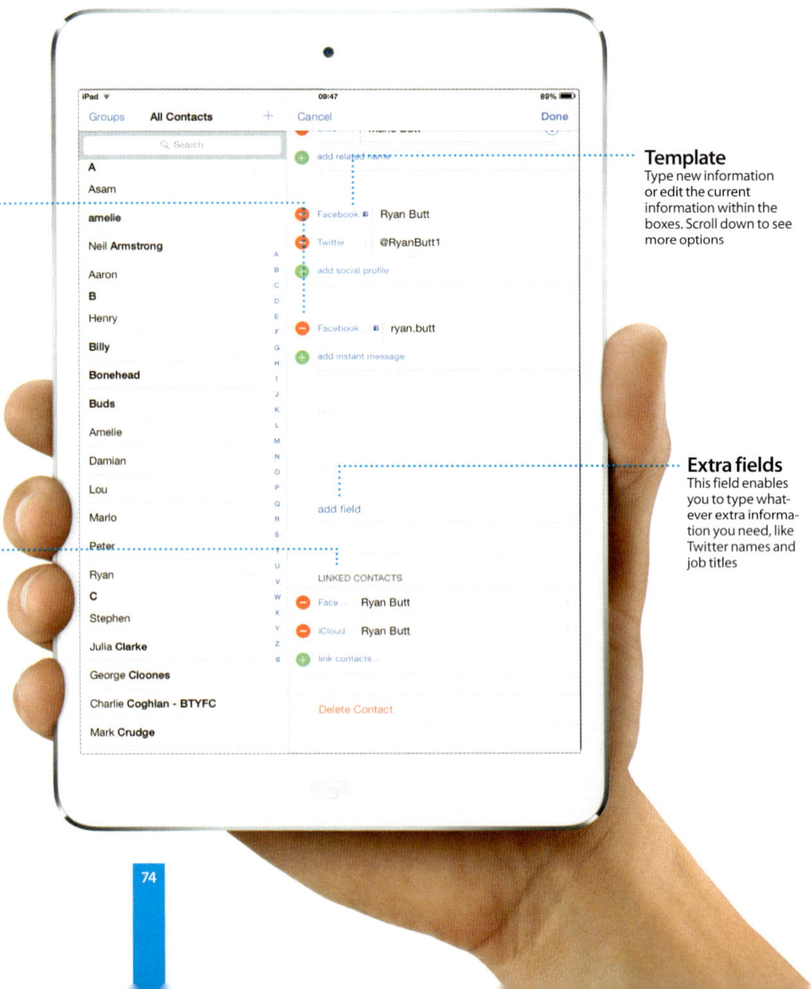

Template
Type new information or edit the current information within the boxes. Scroll down to see more options

Delete info
When editing a contact, press on a red circle to reveal the Delete button, then tap it to clear the field

Extra fields
This field enables you to type whatever extra information you need, like Twitter names and job titles

Linking contacts
Press here in order to link and unlink the contacts that you want this information to be associated with

Before you share your contact, make sure all of the info is correct and edit it if you need to

tapping on it will open the Safari browser and the contents of that website will be displayed. You can also tap on an email address within your contact list to open the Mail app and create a new email to send to that person.

Share a contact

Within each completed Contact page, you have the ability to share the contact. This provides a quick and simple way of sharing details, which is ideal if a contact is packed with information that would take too long to copy or rewrite.

To share your contact, open your desired Contact page and scroll to the base of the page. On the right-hand side of the sheet, tap on the Share Contact button. Two options then appear denoting how you can share that contact information. In this case, Email and Message. Tap on the Email option, for example, and a new email page will appear. Notice that a file icon also exists. This .vcf file contains all of the required information. When you email this file, your recipient can then load it into their Contacts app. All of the information will then be made available to the recipient too, so your Contacts app is a great way of networking.

Share via Message

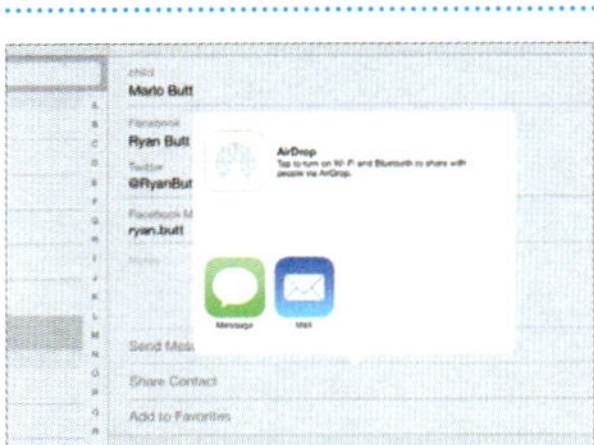

1 Open Contact
Open a contact and scroll to the bottom until you see 'Share Contact'.

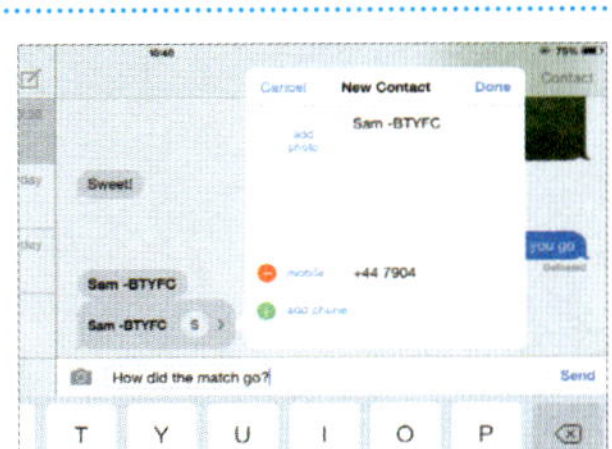

2 Share contact
Tap on Share Contact, select Message, enter the text and then send.

Email a contact card

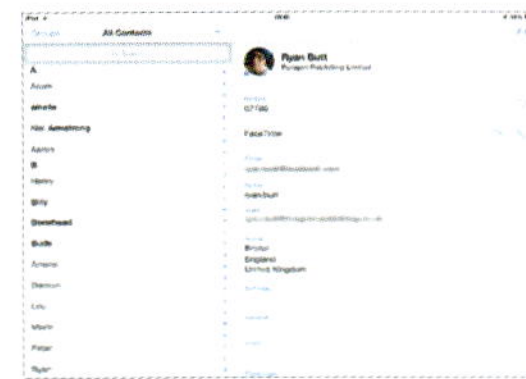

1 Open Contacts
Open the Contacts app and select the contact of choice.

2 Scroll to Contacts
Scroll down until you reach the Share Contact option. Tap on it.

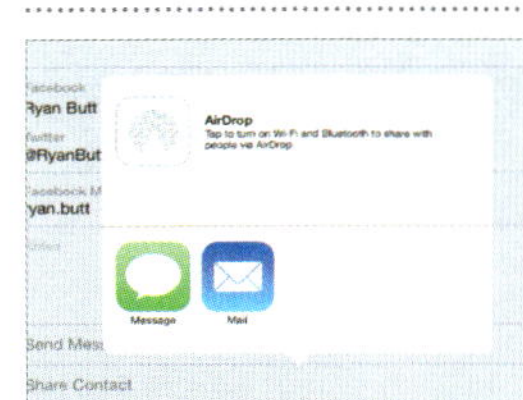

3 New email page
Tap on the Email option and a new email page will appear.

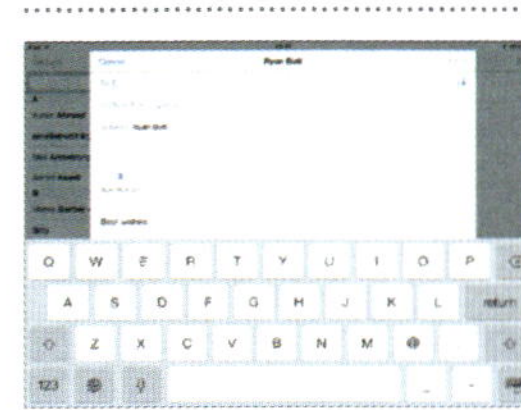

4 Complete email
Complete the email and send to pass on the .vcf file.

Messages

Use the Messaging app and keep in contact with your friends and family

You'll use it to...

Send text messages
Send unlimited text messages to other OS X and iOS devices over Wi-Fi, 3G or 4G

Share photos
You can send photos via a text message

Share videos
Pass your videos on to others

Add attachments
Any attached data can be texted

Have conversations
Your texts can be grouped into a conversation template

Chat with groups
You can send one message to a group of people

Keep in touch using texts

Messaging is one of the most popular activities within the mobile sphere. Using your Messages app, you can send text to one or more people, often simultaneously along with a variety of data attachments, in a similar way to email (Fig 1).

Text using iMessage

The concept of messaging between devices is not unusual but Apple has moved the technology on a step by introducing the iMessage. The difference between the basic text message and the iMessage is that you can begin a conversation on one device and then continue it on another device (Fig 2). For example, you can start an iMessage conversation on your iPhone while travelling on a bus, but then when you get home and you have entered your home office to check a document on your iPad, you can continue the conversation on that device without losing the flow.

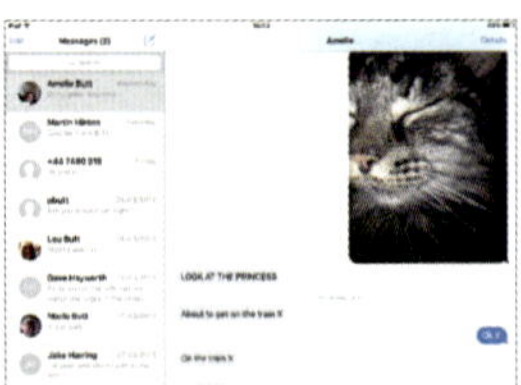

Fig 1 (above) Messages are grouped into conversations to enable you to retain the structure and flow of the chats

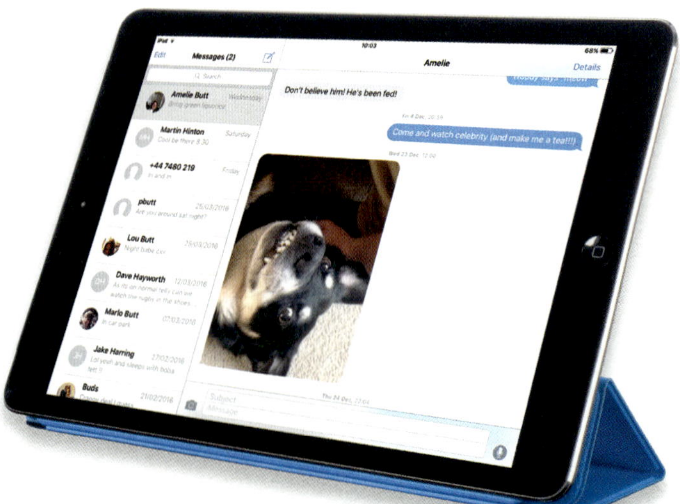

Fig 2 (right) Thanks to iCloud you can begin a conversation on one device and then continue ti on another

As long as the devices are both logged in to the same iCloud account, the conversation will, in fact, be available on all of the iOS devices that you currently own, giving you a high degree of flexibility. If you are concerned about security, be assured that all iMessages are encrypted.

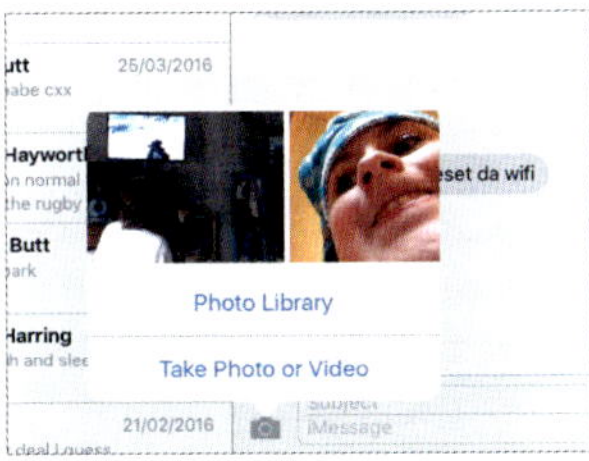

Share photos

One of the highlights of the messaging system is the ability to transfer data along with your text. One of the data types that you can send is the photo. To do that you need to choose your required contact and write a covering note. To choose an image, tap on the camera icon to the left of the message input window and then you can either take a new photo from within the Messages app by selecting the Take Photo or Video option (after which your iPad's Camera app will launch), or import one from your Photos app by selecting the Choose Existing option. If you go for the latter option, scroll through your various photo albums to find the images you wish to attach.

Send locations

One of the unique aspects of messaging is not only having the ability to send an object in the form of data but being able to send links to other data too. Hence, you can send a link to the location of a map, for example.

To do so, open up the Maps app and find the location you wish to share. Press on the location to trigger the banner heading, press the 'i' icon for more information, scroll down the pop-up window and select Share Location. Then, from the sharing menu, choose Message and select the relevant contact.

Sharing your location also reveals a useful distance-from-your-current-location figure

Delete messages

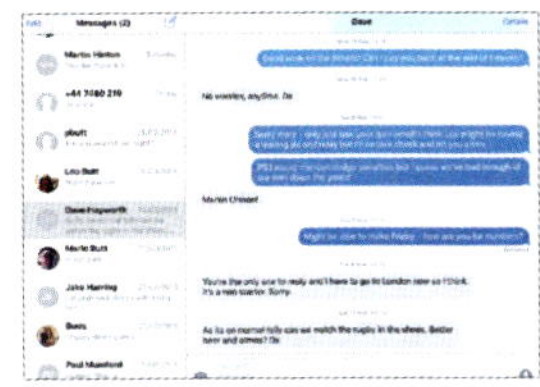

1 Select contact
Find the contact or conversation you want to edit.

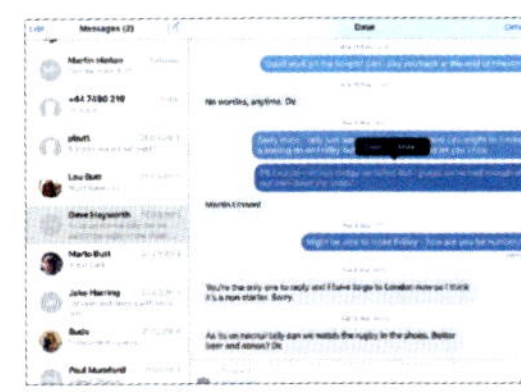

2 Press and hold
Press and hold on the message that you want to delete.

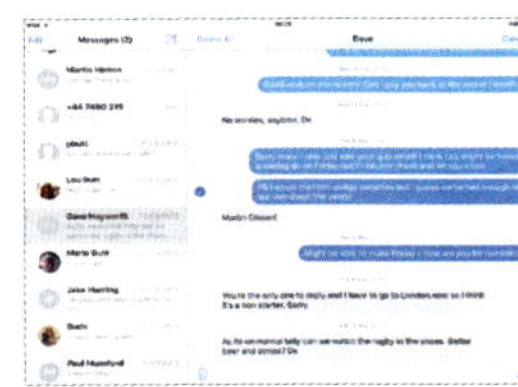

3 Tap More
Tap 'More' on the floating options bar and a tick will appear.

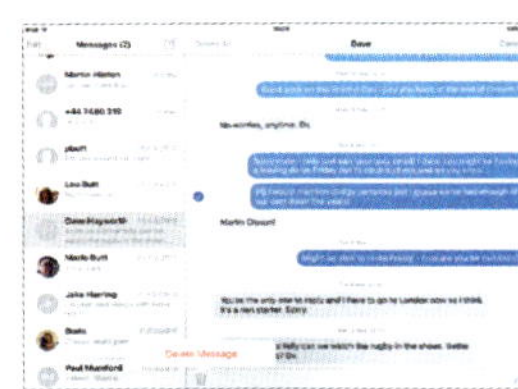

4 Delete message
Now tap on the trash icon to erase the message.

Group messaging

There is an alternative messaging method which can often save time and effort. Your device provides the ability to send a single message to a group of people. To begin, load the Message app and open a new message. Complete the message and press the '+' icon next to the 'To' header at the top of the screen (Fig 3). Your Contacts list will then pop on screen.

This list can be scrolled in order for you to find the group of contacts you wish to choose. Select the first person you wish to send your email, which will be inserted as a sender. Tap the '+' icon again to select another and repeat until your group is complete. If you receive a Message as part of a group chat, the conversation's

Fig 3 When you begin to type in your message, the '+' (Add Contact) icon disappears from view

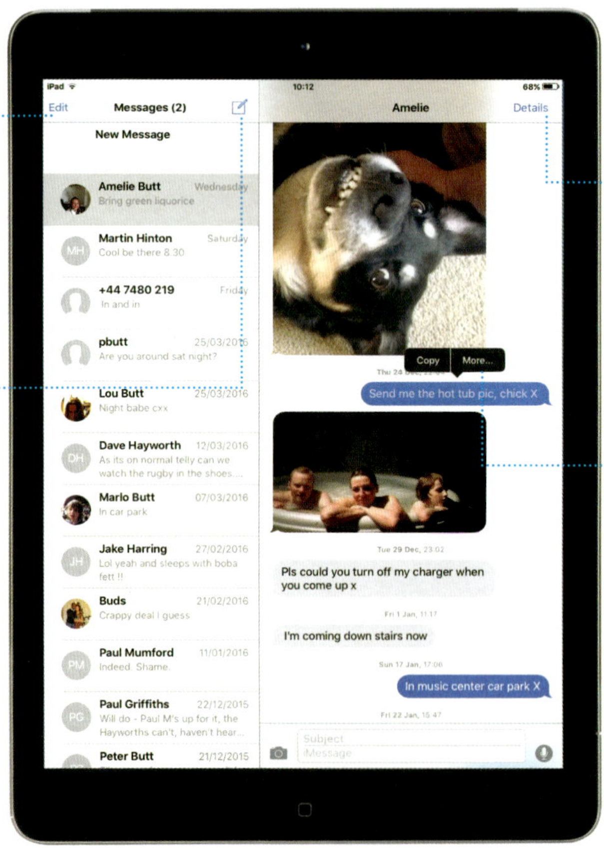

Edit button
Tap this button to erase entire conversations. Press the associated red button and tap Delete

New message
Tap the pad and pencil icon to bring up a new message screen, then type your message

Details
Tap to either send a message, enter a FaceTime conversation or Share a Contact

Delete texts
Press and hold on a message to bring up an option bar, then tap on More to select and delete individual messages

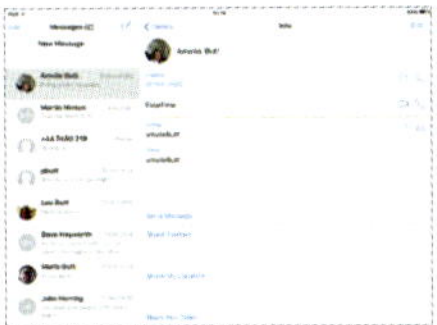

You can share a contact by tapping on Contact, then the 'i' icon and choosing share

entry in the Messages app will have the group icon (which looks like the silhouette of two people) to the left of it. It's easy to tell which participant sent the message, even in a group chat because the person's name will appear above the message itself when you look at the conversation.

Read/delivery receipts

We are all used to sending text messages to colleagues, friends and family and, when the text leaves our phone, we get on with our lives. There are times, however, when an important message is sent and you want to be sure that the other person knows you have read it. This may be because of a business decision or maybe you just want to make sure that the recipient is aware that a message has been read.

On your device, you can turn on the Send Read Receipts option which will provide the sender with an indication that you have received and have read the message. To do this, tap on the Settings app and then scroll the left window until you reach the Messages section. Tap Messages and, on the right, a new window will appear. Now look for the Send Read Receipts option and turn it on.

Enable read receipts

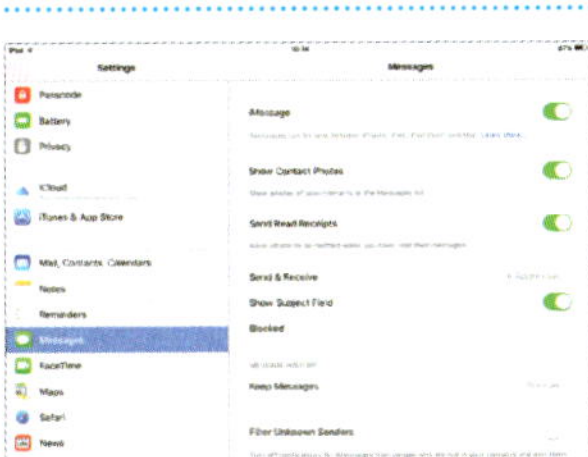

1 Settings
Go to the Settings>Messages and then turn 'Send Read Receipts' to on.

2 Get the confirmation
As soon as your message is read, you'll see confirmation under the message.

Add more addresses

1 Launch Settings
Launch the Settings app from the Home screen of your device.

2 Send & Receive
Go to the Messages section and tap on Send & Receive.

3 Another Email
Choose the option labelled Add Another Email.

4 Type address
Type in the secondary email address you'd like to use.

Reminders

You need never forget to do something ever again with your iPad's built-in memory bank

You'll use it to...

Make lists
Compose lists of tasks to complete

Set reminders
Get alerted when you need to complete particular tasks

Sync to iCloud
Get reminders pushed to other devices

Tick off tasks
A handy check-box lets you tick off items as you complete them

Check your calendar
Reminders syncs with the Calendar app to track your key dates

Remember everything
An intuitive interface means reminding yourself is easy

Set and schedule tasks

Reminders lets you organise your life, setting yourself tasks complete with due dates and lists (Fig 1). The app works with iCloud and your calendar accounts, so any changes that you make will update automatically on all of your iOS devices and computers. It's the simple way to never forget anything ever again!

Set a reminder

Setting yourself a new reminder is a quick and easy process and you can do so by tapping on a line on the page. You will now be prompted to enter a description of your task, so use the pop-up keyboard to summarise your task and then press the down arrow to make the keyboard disappear. You can then fine-tune the settings for the task by tapping on it in the list (Fig 2).

When the Details box appears, tap on the Remind Me button and then move the 'On a Day' slider to the On position. Now tap on the date and you will be able set it to any date and time you

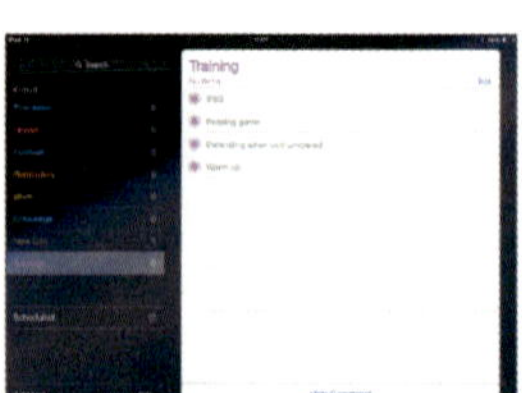

Fig 1 (above) With Reminders you can organise your life into simple 'to-do' lists

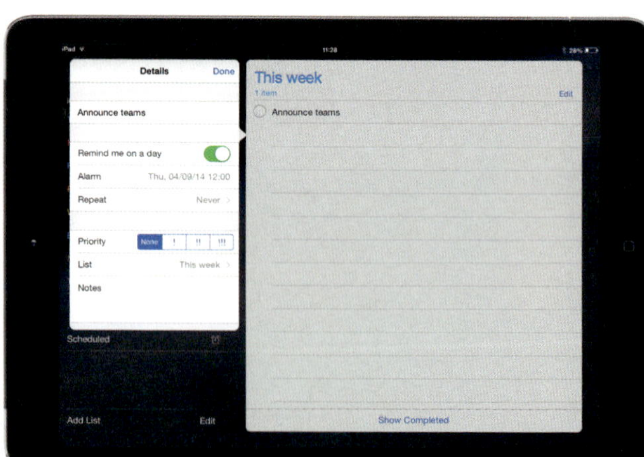

Fig 2 (right) Create a task and tap on it to bring up the Details box and fine-tune the settings

want. Once you have set the remind date, tap Done to return to the Details box and then select the Show More option. Here you can select a list for your reminder to appear on and add any additional notes that you want.

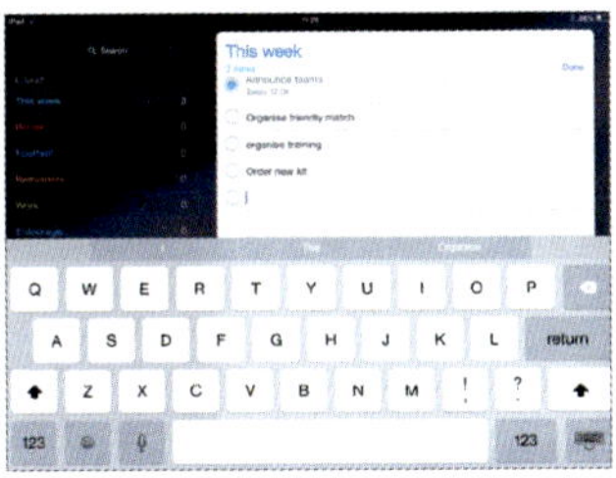

Create lists

Organising reminders into lists makes it easy to keep your work, personal and other to-dos separate from each other. The app comes with one list for active reminders, plus a built-in list of completed items – and you can also add other lists of your own. To create a list, tap on the 'List' tab at the top of the interface and then tap Edit. The option to Create New List will then appear under your various accounts, so tap on one and then type in the preferred name of the list.

Reminders and iCloud

Reminders is just one of many apps that utilises Apple's iCloud service, which means that any lists and tasks that you create in the iCloud section will be synced and pushed to all of your other Apple devices, including iPhones, Macs Apple Watches, completely wirelessly and automatically.

Obviously it might not be possible to carry your iPad around with your everywhere, so to get reminders created on iPad pushed to your iPhone would be useful. Go to Settings and ensure that the Reminders slider is turned on in the iCloud Settings to use this feature. The ability to set location-based reminders is also present so that your device will chime in when you either leave or arrive at a certain address.

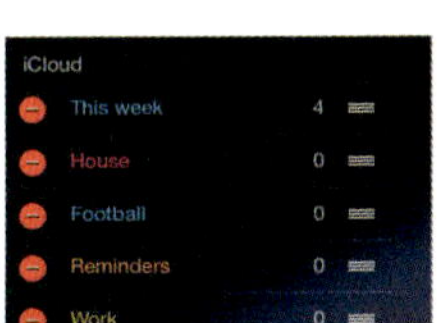

To delete lists, in List view, tap Edit and then hit the red '-' icon for each list you want to delete

Repeat reminders

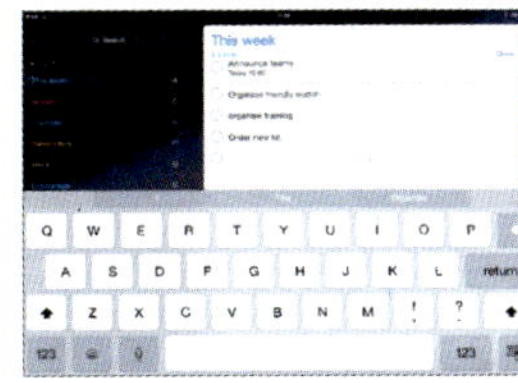

1 Open the app
Open your Reminders app, and tap on a line to add an entry.

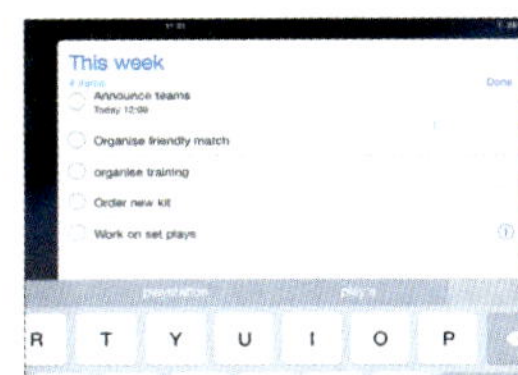

2 Write reminder
You can now write your reminder and it will appear in your list.

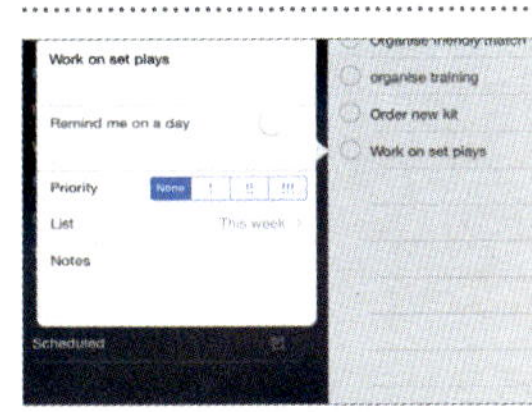

3 Details
Once finished, tap the 'i' icon and it'll bring up the details.

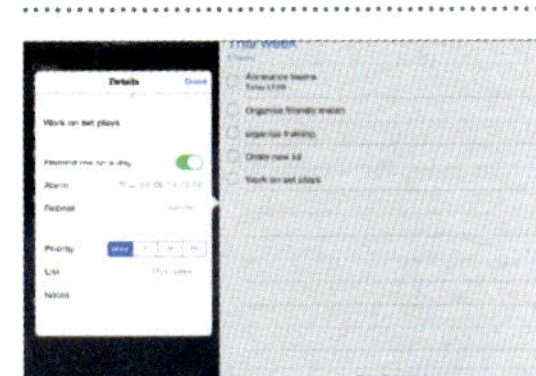

4 Repeat
Turn on Remind Me On a Day to set the reminder to repeat.

Notes

Notes lets you jot down thoughts or ideas, and with iOS 9, you can draw them out with a variety of tools

You'll use it to...

Write down ideas
Jot ideas while you're on the move

Organise automatically
Notes are listed by time and date created

Take advantage of iCloud
Share your notes and information

Keep note accounts
Create a note-specific account

Search your notes
Search the app for a specific note

Print and email
You can print your notes via AirPlay

Take notes with ease

The Notes app is the perfect way to quickly write down those ideas, lists and anything else that pops into your head that you may need to remember later on (Fig 1). With iOS 9, your notemaking is made easier, and more instinctive, through the addition of several writing and drawing tools, like a pen, pencil and marker in various colours.

Write and share notes

Notes are now categorised in folders on your iPad. You can create a new folder by tapping the option at the bottom of the left column on your iPad. Then create a new note with the icon in the top right. Every note is presented in an easily accessible list and is simple to share from within the app itself.

To start sharing your notes, tap the Sharing icon that's located at the top-right of the screen (indicated by an arrow in a box) and you will then be presented with options to Email, Message, Copy or

Fig 1 (above) Notes provides plenty of screen space for you to write down and store a whole range of information

Fig 2 (right) You can easily share your Notes in a variety of different ways

Print (Fig 2). If you opt to email your note, the contents of the current note will be copied and pasted into an email. All you have to do then is add the recipient's address in the correct field and you can mail it straight out from within the Notes app. There's no need to cut, paste and switch between the apps yourself. You can print your notes wirelessly, and Notes is also iCloud compatible. Any notes you create can be accessed on all iOS devices.

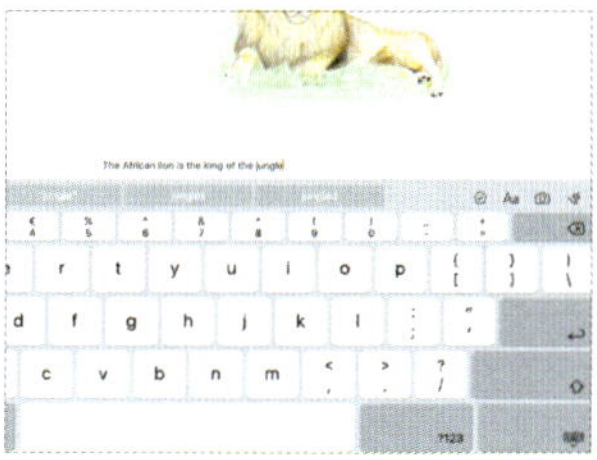

Keyboard tricks

There are plenty of tricks and shortcuts on your iPad that you can also use to your advantage. Pressing the space bar twice in quick succession will place a full stop and a space at the end of your sentence. Also, press and hold on the numbers key and quickly slide your finger to the number or symbol you wish to place before taking your finger off – it will switch back to the letters keyboard, allowing you to continue typing. To get a quick apostrophe, tap and hold the '!' button and slide your finger upwards.

Notes and iCloud

Notes can be linked to the iCloud. This gives you the ability to access your notes via different platforms such as a MacBook, iPhone and iMac as well as your iPad. If you use a **me.com** or **mac.com** email address for iCloud, go to the Settings and tap on iCloud and turn on Notes. If you use a Gmail or other web email account for iCloud, go to the Settings app and tap on the Mail option then tap Contacts and Calendars. Then turn on Notes for the account. All of these features enhance your Notes experience and make note-taking as simple as possible.

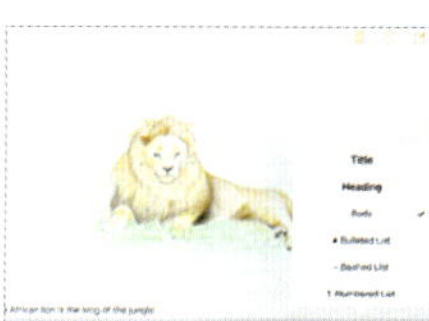

Change titles and font types by pressing the 'Aa' button at the top of your new keyboard

Start drawing in Notes

1 Open Notes
iOS 9 lets you organise notes in folders. Open and name one.

2 Drawing and tools
Tap the squiggly line to start drawing with the tools available.

3 Pencil
Use the pencil, which acts like a real one, to start the basics.

4 Pen and zoom
Pinch the screen to zoom in, and add optional details with the pen.

Maps

Use the Maps app to search for and find directions to a location in both graphical or textual form

You'll use it to...

Enter a search
Search for and find your chosen location

Driving
Get a great series of driving directions

Flyover
Obtain a 3D, aerial flyover view

Zoom in
Double-tap on a map to zoom in

More info
Press on a label to find out more info

Print
Print out a useful set of directions straight from your device

Find your way around the world

Maps on provides you with a real-time map that can offer turn-by-turn directions that are spoken by your device. Alongside this there are interactive 3D views plus an amazing Flyover feature. The entire world is open for examination.

Navigating Maps

The Maps app has enjoyed several new iOS 9 enhancements to make it even easier to navigate between locations and discover what's around you. Whereas previously the directions given through the Maps app focused on car journeys and journeys by foot, the enhanced iOS 9 version allows you to use public transport with Maps as your guide. In selected cities around the workd, a new 'Transit' view displays all of the train lines and stations for trains, metros, buses and even ferries. What's more, if you are trying to get around places that don't feature the 'Transit' view, this will be replaced by an 'Apps' option. Tapping on this will provide quite links

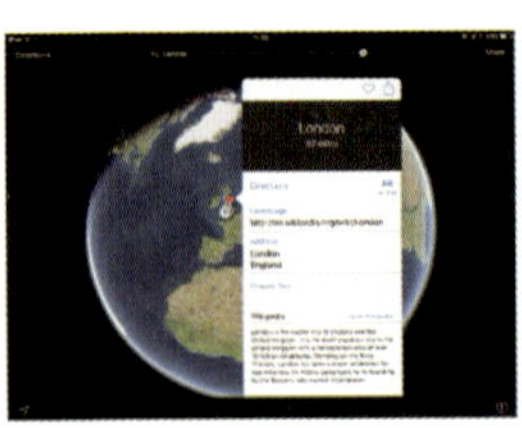

Fig 1 (above) If you want to jump between global points, it's easy to rotate the Earth over multiple axes

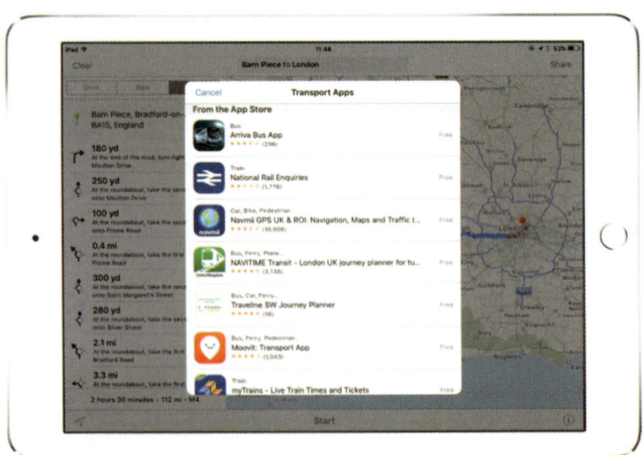

Fig 2 (right) The items located in your search are highlighted by red pins

to a selection of apps that will help you on your journey (Fig 2). You can download these third-party apps from within the Maps app and, once installed, tap on the 'Route' option to have thew third-party app map out your desired route.

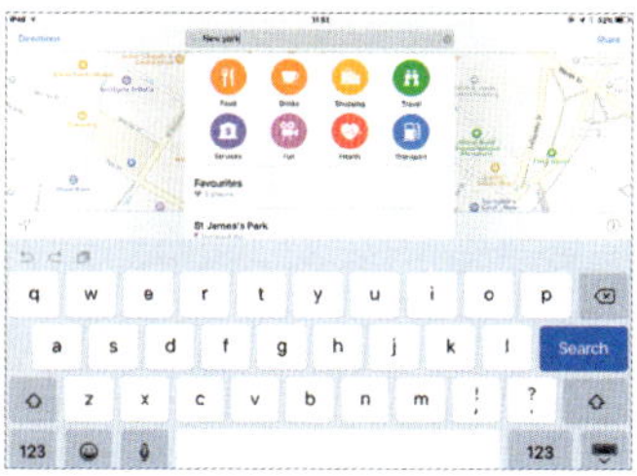

What's nearby?

While exploring a destination, the new Nearby feature, accessible by tapping on the Search field at the top of the interface, will show you a list of quick categories, including Food, Drinks, Shopping, Services, Fun and Health. Tap on a category to get a rundown of more in-depth listings. For example, under 'Food' you will be treated to a list of popular restaurants, grocery stores, fast food outlets and cafés. This feature makes it incredibly easy to get your bearings and see all nearby places of interest upon arriving at a strange city. Additionally, iOS 9 now offers public transport info in certain cities.

Get directions

Once you have found your required location, press on the pin to reveal the banner. Then press the Directions button on the top left-hand corner of the screen. A drop-down window will reveal your chosen location and three modes of transport: Drive, Walk and, if applicable, Transit (if not, Apps). Once you have selected how you want to travel a visual route will appear on the map and each individual step of the journey will be displayed in a list to the left. You will often be presented with multiple routes to the same destination (alternate routes will be displayed as less-prominent blue lines on the map), so tap on an alternative if required.

Tap the compass point icon in the lower-left corner to jump straight to your current location

Bookmark a place

1 Route
Select your start and end point and then tap on Route.

2 End point
Press on your final location to reveal a banner.

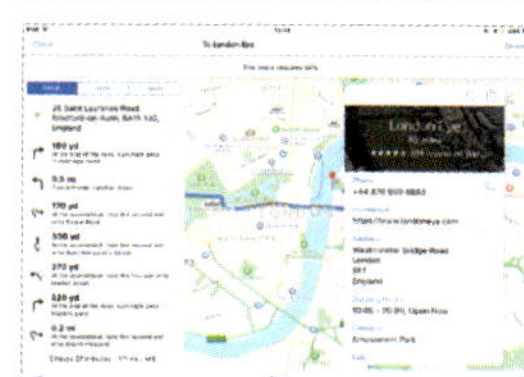

3 Information
Press the 'i' icon to see further information about the location.

4 Bookmark
Tap on the heart icon at the top of the menu to save the spot.

Clock

Keep track of the time wherever you are in the world and never be late again with the Clock app

You'll use it to…

Browse world times
See the time in cities across the globe

Set an alarm
Have different alarms for numerous tasks

Measure elapsed time
Use the stopwatch and see time go by

Measure time intervals
See the time left between tasks

Catch the latest news
The clock links to Yahoo! in your location

Check the weather
View summaries of local climates

Keep track of time

As well as letting you see the time across the world (Fig 1), the Clock app also allows you to time the interval between events or use a stopwatch. It also operates as a brilliant alarm clock with the possibility of setting multiple alerts.

Set an alarm

When you tap the '+' icon in the top right-hand corner, you are able to begin setting an alarm (Fig 2). Use the dials to configure the exact time by scrolling up and down using your fingers until you find the right one. You can then decide whether or not you want to repeat the alarm, which you can do on any day of the week, and whether or not you would like to include a snooze function.

It is possible to label that particular alarm with any name you wish. For example, you could decide that you would like to label one 'Waking up' and another one for a meeting.

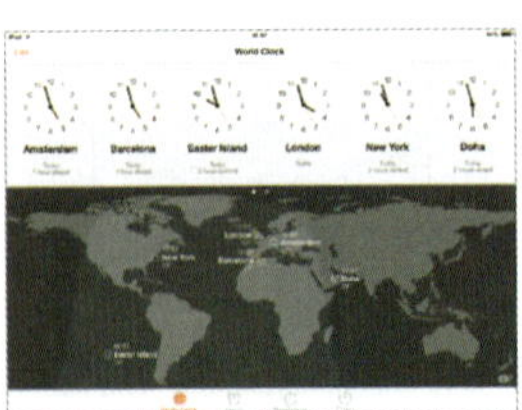

Fig 1 (above) You can add pages and pages of world times – just tap Add

Fig 2 (right) Tap the '+' icon in order to begin setting up your alarms for various different tasks

It is also possible to add a particular sound to your alarm. When you have completed this, the alarm will show on the calendar within the Clock app so that you can see, at a glance, when any of your alarms have been set. It is possible to edit any of these by selecting Edit in the top left-hand corner.

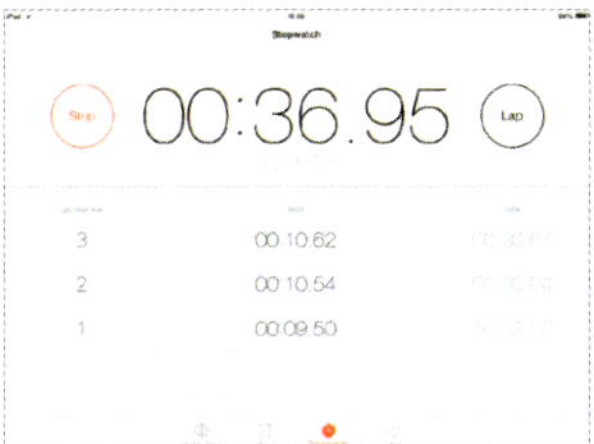

Stopwatch and timers

When you tap on the Stopwatch tab at the bottom of the screen, you are able to begin measuring elapsed time. Likewise, when you select Timer, you can measure time intervals as well.

With the Stopwatch, you simply tap Start and the time will begin to increase. When you tap Stop, it will cease. The Stopwatch has a great lap timer, too. Tapping Lap when a lap is finished will show the time that the lap took to complete.

On the Timer, simply input the timescale you want using the dials and then tap Start. The countdown begins.

World clocks

As well as being able to see a set of five default time zones of Cupertino, New York, Paris, Beijing and Tokyo, tapping Add lets you find any location around the world and see the exact time at that particular location too.

When you tap the Add button, you will be shown a list of included time zones. You can either scroll through these and find one that you want, or you can decide instead to use the keyboard and input a search term. Tap the result you are looking for and the clock will be added to those that already exist. The time will also be placed on the world map.

You can quickly turn off your alarms by going to Alarm and moving the slider to the Off position

Add music to an alarm

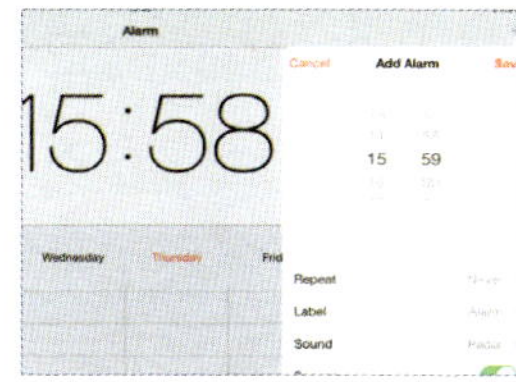

1 Add alarm
Tap on '+' to Add Alarm. You will then need to select Sound.

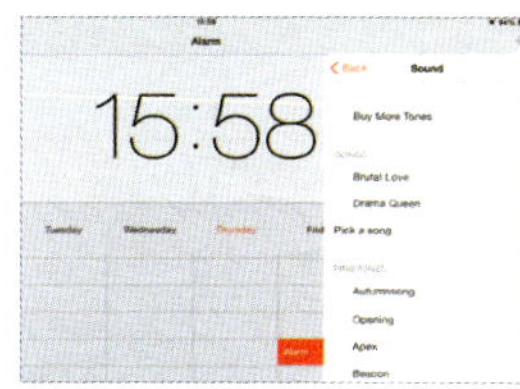

2 Select song
In the Songs category, some of your tunes will be listed.

3 Pick a song
Either tap one of these options or, alternatively, select Pick a song.

4 Search for tunes
When you have found one you want to use, tap it to choose it.

FaceTime

FaceTime is ideal for talking to your friends, family or colleagues in real time via video link

You'll use it to…

Make video calls
Talk face-to-face with friends and family

Talk to other devices
Call from iPad to iPhone or MacBook

Switch cameras
Easily switch from front to rear cameras

Call for free
FaceTime calls are free of charge

Use FaceTime on TV
Great for making group calls

Add Favourites
Create FaceTime favourites

Fig 1 (above) You can easily control the volume during a FaceTime call

Fig 2 (right) Make sure FaceTime is turned on in the Settings app first

Chat face-to-face

FaceTime allows you to undertake video calls with another user of a compatible Apple device absolutely free over a 4G or WiFi network. The app also includes a picture-in-picture facility while you're talking, so that you can see how you look to the person on the other end of the call.

Call a contact with FaceTime

To enable you to use FaceTime, you will initially need to activate the feature in the Settings app and set up an Apple ID, if you haven't already obtained one. You'll also need a Wi-Fi or cellular 4G connection for the app to work (Fig 2).

When you open FaceTime, you may be prompted to sign in using your Apple ID or create a new account. Before you can make your FaceTime call, tap the Contacts app and find the details of the person you are planning to call. Choose a name and either tap that person's phone number or their email address. Either option

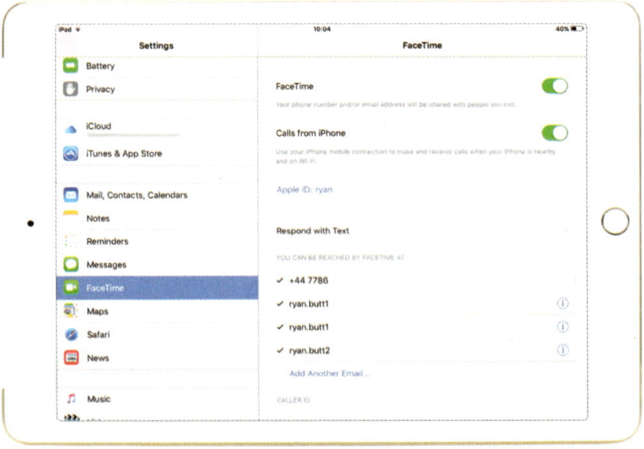

will open FaceTime. When making the call, you can hold the iPad in either landscape or portrait orientation. It is advisable, however, to lock the rotation before you make your call to avoid disruptive orientation changes during your chat.

The FaceTime interface lets you switch between Video calls or Audio calls via the tabs at the top of the interface. Audio calls are essentially just like regular phone calls, but free between iOS users.

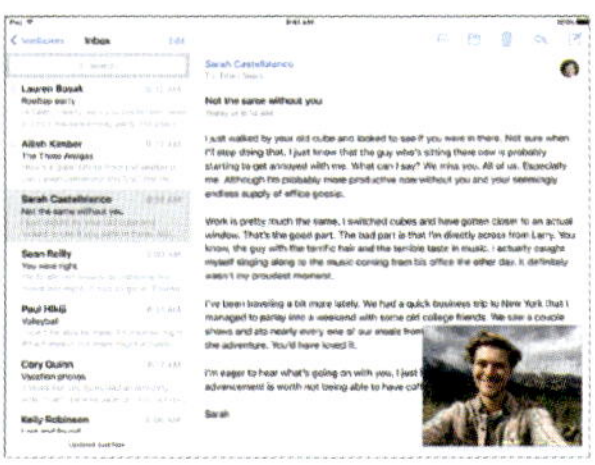

Picture in picture

One of the iOS 9 enhancements made to FaceTime was the inclusion of picture in picture mode. This means that you can reduce the size of your FaceTime window on your iPad screen so as to carry out other tasks while you chat. To enable PiP mode, simply tap on the PiP icon in the lower corner of your chat window. You can drag the reduced FaceTime window around to reposition and place your fingers on it and pinch/expand to change the size of the window. It's a new way to never let chat get in the way of work.

Chat on multiple devices

One of the more useful features of the FaceTime app is its capacity to be used in between devices, for example iPad and iPhone, iPad and iMac and iPad and MacBook. This is a real bonus, as you can initiate a new conversation no matter where you are and what you're doing – so long as you have an Apple device on you.

There are slight differences in how communication is initiated, however. The requirement of an Apple ID is constant but, in addition, you will need a phone number if you want to call an iPhone. To call an iPad, iPod touch or Mac, you can use an email.

To remove favourites from FaceTime, tap the Edit button, select the contact and hit Delete

The FaceTime controls

1 Picture in picture
Look at the small image of yourself that your caller sees.

2 Show what you're seeing
Toggle the camera view with the bottom-left camera icon.

3 Mute your speech
Mute yourself with the bottom right mute icon.

4 End call
To end the call, press the End button situated bottom-centre.

Camera

With the iPad's powerful camera, you can take and process photographs on the go

You'll use it to...

Capture images
Take and process photos quickly, efficiently and easily

View multiple images
Browse through many photos at the same time on the iPad's screen

Record and edit video
Take moving pictures and trim them down to shorten the length

Share photos
Transfer images to other devices with the iPad's network capabilities

Upload to YouTube
Publish your videos online straight from the app with the upload function

Capture stunning images

The Camera app provides all the necessary tools that you require to take striking and impressive photographs. In addition, you can collate images and store them for future viewing, manage images into albums and share them with friends and family via both Wi-Fi and 4G.

Manage and edit your images

The built-in Photos app lets you view photos that you capture on your iPad, or those you've synced to it. Photos that you take with the built-in camera or save from an email, text message, webpage or screenshot are all included here (Fig 1).

To view images, just tap one of the buttons at the bottom of the screen. For example, tap the Album button and then a specific album to see its full suite of thumbnails. Tap a thumbnail image to see the photo itself. You can also use the pinch gesture command

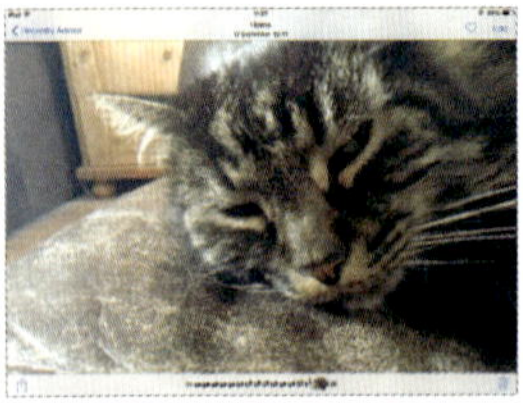

Fig 1 (above) Take and organise your favourite photos for later viewing

Fig 2 (right) Adding filter effects to your image provides a range of impressive-looking results

to open or close an album, view a photo or go back to the thumbnail view.

To edit a photo, display your chosen image and tap on Edit on the top right. A selection of commands will be listed at the side of the screen. You can Rotate and Enhance the image at the tap of a button, and also make Red-Eye correction. Tap filters to display a range of additional filter tools that add visual effects (Fig 2). Crop provides aspect ratio measurements to trim your image.

Access viewfinder features

One of the principal features in the Camera app is the HDR (High Dynamic Range) button. On the app's viewer screen, tap to turn on HDR and, when you press the trigger button, the iPad will blend the best of three instant exposures into an improved single photo.

Swipe the menu to Square and the output image will adopt a square shape – ideal for sharing on Instagram. Finally, you can use gesture movements to zoom in and out of the viewer.

Share your images

Photos are automatically uploaded to My Photo Stream and then spread to the rest of your enabled devices, whether iPhone, MacBook or iMac. To turn on My Photo Stream, go to Settings>iCloud>Photos>My Photo Stream. New photos that you have taken are uploaded to My Photo Stream when you leave the Camera app and when your iPad is connected to the internet via Wi-Fi or 4G. To save photos to your iPad from My Photo Stream, go to the Photo Stream album, tap Select (top right) to select the photos that you wish to save, tap Add To and then select the save destination.

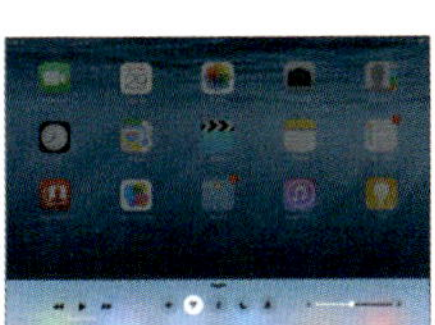

To start Camera quickly, swipe up the Control Centre and tap the Camera icon

Take a photo

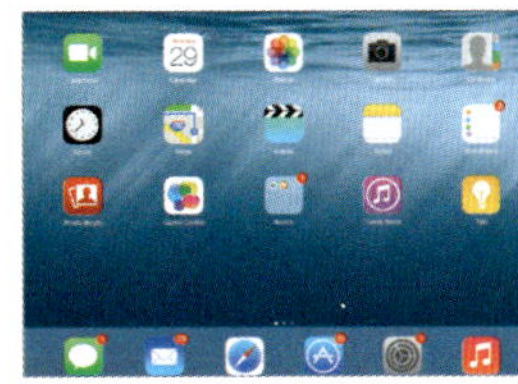

1 Select Camera
From the Home page, tap the Camera app.

2 Select Photo
On the right, swipe the menu choice to Photo or Square.

3 Prepare to snap
Wait briefly for the yellow, auto-focus, box to appear on-screen.

4 Take and save
Press the white button. A shutter noise indicates a saved image.

Camera

Fig 3 Trim your new video to size during the editing process

Record and edit a video

To take a video, open up the Camera app. Make sure that the Camera/Video/Square selector to the right is set to the Video mode. To do this, swipe it to the video position.

Lift the iPad and aim it at your chosen subject. Make sure that you frame your subject and pause a second, allowing the iPad to focus (a rectangle briefly appears to show that both the exposure and focus are now set). Tap on the red video trigger button that is situated within the screen, halfway up on the right hand side. The video will begin and a sound effect will be triggered to indicate this. Press again to stop and save.

Main screen
The largest area of the screen is where video plays on the iPad. Here, you can compose your film

Mode select
Swipe the mode to select Camera, Video or Square, which turns the window into a square shape

Shutter delay
Tap this icon to choose a shutter delay from three or ten seconds to line up your perfect shot

Camera switch
At the top right, the camera switch icon will toggle the front and rear facing cameras

In video mode, quickly access your last video by tapping the thumbnail icon in the bottom-right

You can then edit your footage. Open Photos, tap on Videos and select your video. Notice the bar at the top of the screen containing the video frames. Tap and hold the right side of the frame bar until the Trim command appears (Fig 3). Two yellow lines appear on the right and left side of the frame bar. Press and drag the lines left and right until your video has reached the correct size. Only those frames within the two bars will be saved.

Publish videos on YouTube

You can share a video with the world by uploading it to YouTube almost immediately. If you have something you want to share, tap the Photos app and, when it has opened up, locate and tap on the Videos folder. A selection of your videos will then appear on the screen. Tap on Select at the top right of the screen. Select the video to upload by tapping on it.

Press the Share icon on the top left of the screen. This will reveal a range of icons. Press the YouTube icon and a new YouTube window will appear on the screen. Type in your YouTube username and password. A range of information can then be inserted, including the video title, description, definition information, category and target audience. When ready, tap on Publish.

Shoot a video

1 Select Video
Slide the camera mode to Video and the shutter button will turn red.

2 Start recording
Tap the red button and the clock will display the duration of your film.

Time a photo

1 Tap the timer
Press the clock (timer) icon to the right of the screen.

2 Set the delay
Choose the time delay from the two options available.

3 Line up your shot
With a three or ten-second delay selected, line up your shot.

4 Tap the shutter
Tap the shutter and the picture will be taken after the time.

Photos

Use Photos to organise, edit, view and share your collection of pictures

You'll use it to...

View photos
Browse the photographs stored on your iPad

Enhance photos
Fix faults such as red-eye, brightness and contrast flaws

Create albums
Create albums and add a collection of pictures to them

Watch slideshows
Select albums and watch a slideshow of the photos

Share with friends
Send photos to friends by email and share them online

Turn on Photo Stream
View photos from any device using iCloud and Photo Stream

View your images

Photos look great even on old iOS devices, but they are stunning on models with a retina display, like the newer iPads. There are several ways to browse the photos you have taken, for example tap Albums at the bottom, select an album and then choose a photo to view it.

The Camera Roll

When you take photographs on your iPad, they are automatically saved to an album called Camera Roll. The idea is that it is like an old film camera and the images are organised by date from oldest to newest. Unlike film cameras, your iPad can store hundreds of photos. To view them, press Albums at the bottom of the screen and then tap Camera Roll. Many apps that provide photo functions, such as camera apps, collage makers and so on, work with Camera Roll, either loading photos from it for editing or saving photos to it after modification. It will probably be the part of the Photos app that you use the most. To view a photo just tap it, and to browse

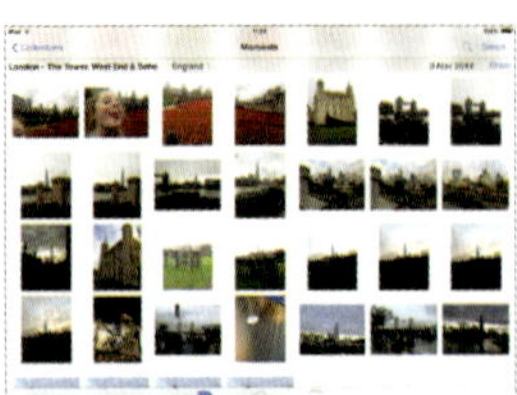

Fig 1 (above) Tap the photo to remove the top and bottom bars and view it full screen

Fig 2 (right) Swipe up and down to browse the Camera Roll and tap photos to view them

through them swipe left or right to see the previous or next image. Not only are photos stored in the Camera Roll, but videos too. They have a video camera icon and length displayed on them.

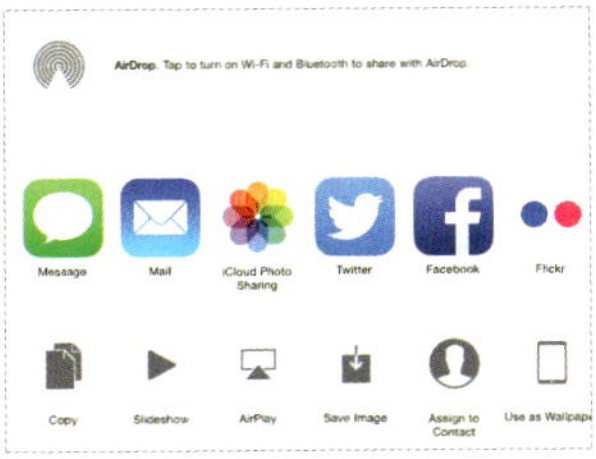

AirPlay

Although your iPad can display your photos and they look fantastic, it isn't so good when you want to show them off to a group of people. A much better solution is to gather everyone around the television and show the photos on that. If you have an Apple TV, pressing the Share button in the corner when viewing a photo provides access to AirPlay. Press it and select Apple TV.

iCloud Photo Library

Many people have more than one Apple device and you might have an iPad, iPhone, Mac and so on. It would be nice to view photos taken on an iPhone on the bigger screen of your iPad, or to see iPad photos on a big screen desktop computer. The iCloud Photo Library is the answer because now every photo that you take is automatically uploaded to your iCloud, giving you freedom to access your library from any device, anytime you want. Go to the Photos & Camera section in your Settings app to configure it.

Slideshows

View any album and there is a Slideshow button in the top-right corner and this is a great way to view your photos. It shows each picture full screen for a few seconds before automatically moving on to the next one. If you have a stand for the iPad, it turns it into a superb animated photo frame. Press the Slideshow button

You can turn on Photo Stream by going to Settings and select Photos & Camera

Create a new album

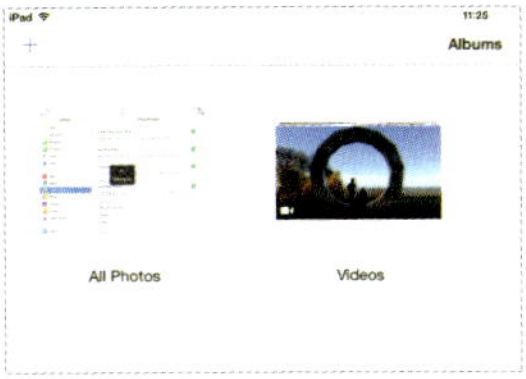

1 My Albums
Press Albums at the bottom, then tap the '+' in the top corner.

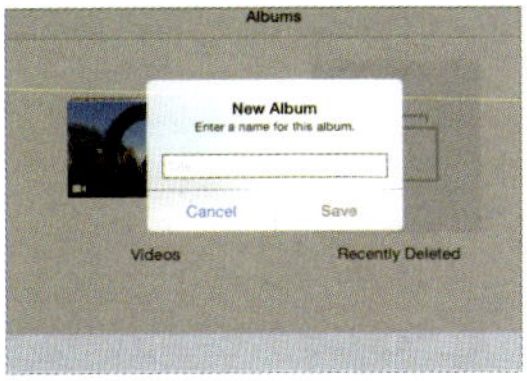

2 Name it
Every album needs a title. Think of a name and press Save.

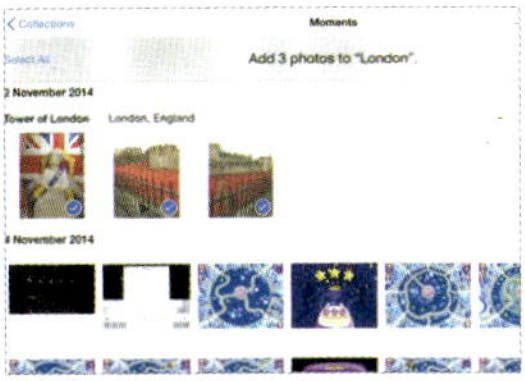

3 Add photos
Select the photos to add to the album and then press Done.

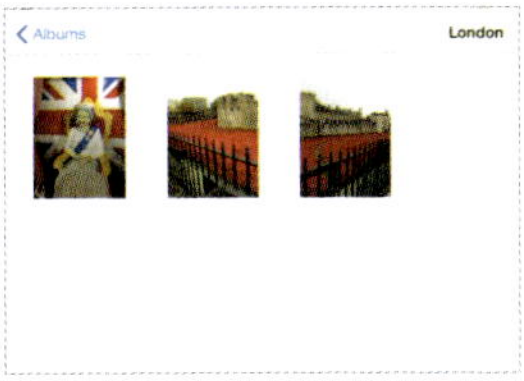

4 View it
You'll end up back at step one, and tapping the album displays it.

Photos

Fig 3 Choose the transitions, select your favourite music and then play the slideshow

and a panel is displayed containing some useful options. For example, there are a number of transitions (special effects) that can be applied when moving to the next photo. Tap the option and choose from Dissolve, Ripple, Wipe and others. Try each one and see which one you like best. It is also possible to play music alongside your slideshow. There are more options to be found by going to Settings on the Home screen and selecting Photos & Camera. You can choose the length of time to display photos and the default is three seconds. You can also choose whether to shuffle the photos or play them in order, and whether to stop after the last one or to repeat the slideshow by going back to the beginning again. Try the slideshows with different settings to see which suits.

Organise your photos
Photos are organised into years, collections and moments based on their date. Select them using this button

Select a photo
Press a photo to view it full screen. Using Select at the top right, multiple photos can be selected

Photos vs Albums
Photos is a different way of viewing your snapshots and it's like an organised view of Camera Roll

Share a moment
This view is Moments, which are small groups of photos. Press Share to share a whole moment

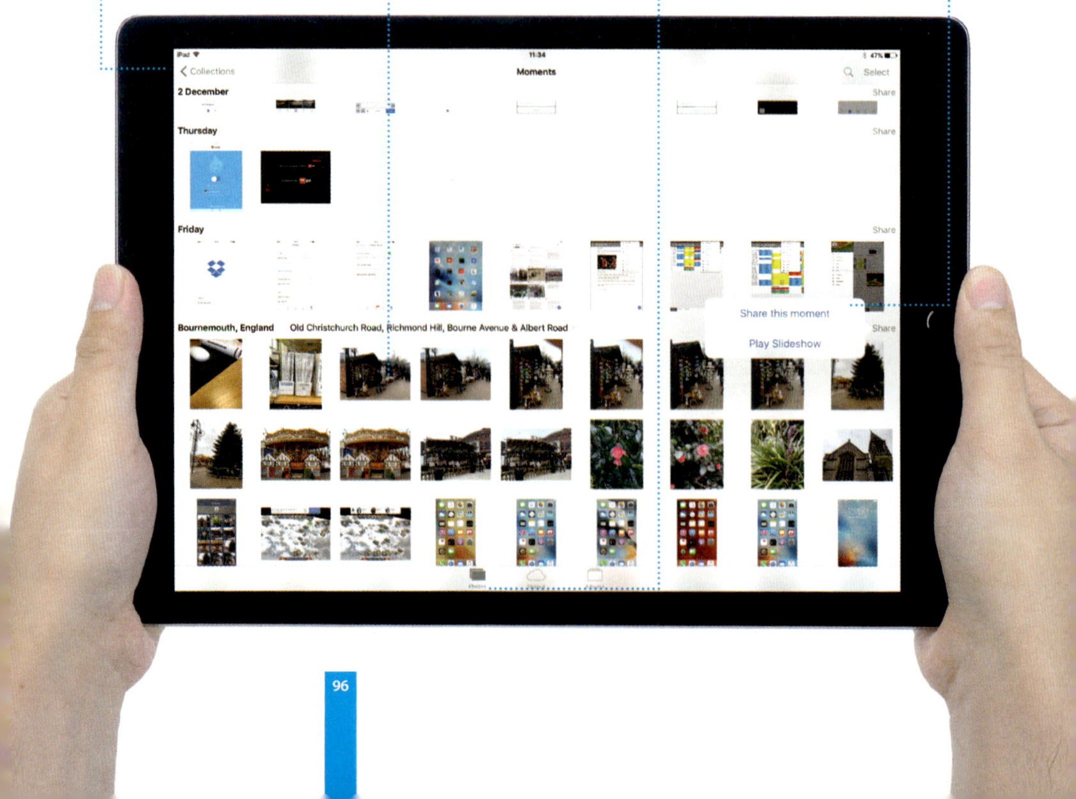

When using Crop, tap the Aspect Ratio icon to choose square, widescreen and so on

Edit photos

Not every photo taken will be perfect. You'll find that some could do with brightening up, a flash may cause someone to have red-eye, or there is too much wasted space that you don't want in the frame. The Photos app has some simple but effective tools for enhancing photographs and fixing minor problems that could otherwise spoil them.

Select a photo and press the Edit button at the top to switch to Edit Photo mode. At the side of the screen is a collection of useful tools, such as Crop, which allows you to trim excess flab and make slight adjustments to the orientation of the image. The Enhance tool is very simple, and one tap is all it takes to adjust the brightness, contrast and saturation. Photos selects the best settings and applies them automatically. The Filters button applies special effects like Mono, Tonal, Fade, Instant and others. Thumbnails are displayed at the bottom and you just tap the one you want. Finally, the dial icon lets you make slight adjustments to the lighting and colour levels of any image. Pick one of the options and then move the slider across the image to see instant changes. Once you have finished editing, tap Done and then changes will be saved.

Enhance photos

1 Auto-enhance
This photo was a bit dull, but pressing Enhance brightened it up.

2 Apply filters
Press Filters and there are interesting effects, like this one that ages photos

Share an image

1 Pick a photo
Open an album and select a photo. Tap the Share button.

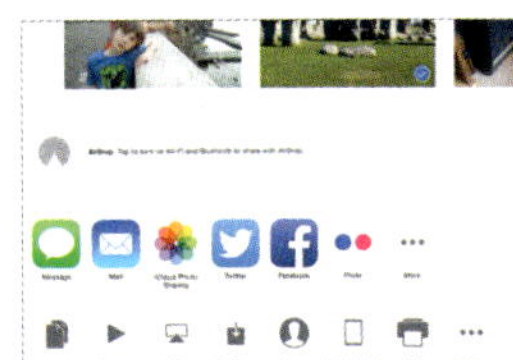

2 Sharing options
There are lots of ways to share items. Tap the one you want.

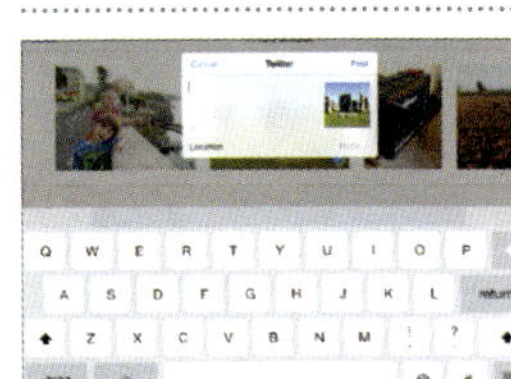

3 Tweet it
Press Twitter or Facebook and enter a comment to the photo.

4 Email it
You can also attach the image into an email if you wish.

Paper by 53

Write and draw with exceptional realism with the creative app Paper by 53

You'll use it to...

Make notes
By simply using your finger or stylus, start writing into the app as if it was a notepad

Sketch out ideas
For many creatives, using Paper by 53 is a great way to pre-empt a final piece of work

Draw plans
If you're doing home improvements, you start sketching out plans there and then

Create charts
Various brushes allow you to create pie charts, bar charts and other graphs

Share images
Share images to the public stream to be edited, and collaborated with other Paper users around the world

Fig 1 (above) Your brushes and mixing pallets are available from your blank canvas, as soon as you open the app.

Fig 2 (right) The app caters to all kinds of drawing styles

Sketch on the go

Paper, the illustrating app from 53, is perfect for sketching ideas and creating finalised pieces of art while on the go, or focused at your desk. With the lifelike rendering of various ink and pencil tips, Paper can generate results that look almost indistinguishable from a real drawing while utilising other aspects of image editing such as a Go Back option to allow you to undo steps and customise your colour pallet, as well as the ability to import photos for annotation.

Use a stylus

Being a versatile addition to any creative's iOS device, paper will allow you to use your finger tip to paint, draw, sketch or write. Alternatively, you can use the app to connect a stylus for a more realistic experience. Styluses can come in a range of styles and designs to best fit your individual requirements, be it size or weight, but no matter which you use, the way Paper handles the interaction is geared to be as realistic and lifelike as possible, meaning sensitive

drawing movements like tilting your pencil to shade in large areas, for example, will be mirrored in the app via it recognising the duration and speed of your movement, so the lighter you press the stylus tip means the lighter the shade of the pencil mark.

Import images

As stated earlier, you can import images from either your device's camera or from your photo stream. This is an especially handy feature if you want to annotate a collaborative piece of art, or directions, but by using the Spotlight feature, you can selectively colour an area of the image to draw attention to that part of the image, or, you can resize the image. Another perk to importing imagery into Paper, is the opportunity it gives you to paint and draw on the top of your image.

Getting colourful

Paper also has a hue and saturation control at the ready which works as a mixer pallet and a slide dial. You can simply select a colour from your pre select swatches, or you can click on the mixer to bring up the hue and saturation, as well as this, you can mix in a secondary colour, adding to the tone, or you can reduce the tone bringing the colour back to its more original state.

Creating graphical representation

If you are a little more plan-oriented and looking to illustrate the layout of your latest project, you can create fairly accurate ellipses, circles, squares, rectangles and triangles using the newly added graph pen. This tool operates as a normal ink pen, but if you draw a triangle and join the points, paper will instantly convert it into a more accurate version of the shape.

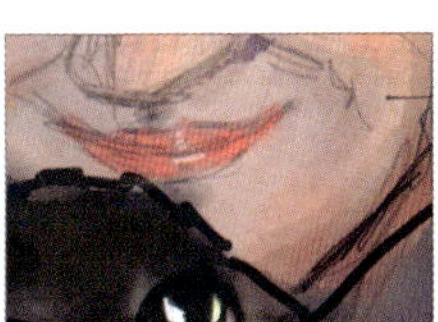

Pinch zoom your image to reveal a dotted grid to help you keep a sense of scale when zooming

Sketch over an image

1 Start with a blank canvas
You will see a camera icon, this will allow you to import an image.

2 Paint in the spaces
Select the image and the paint brush and sketch over the image.

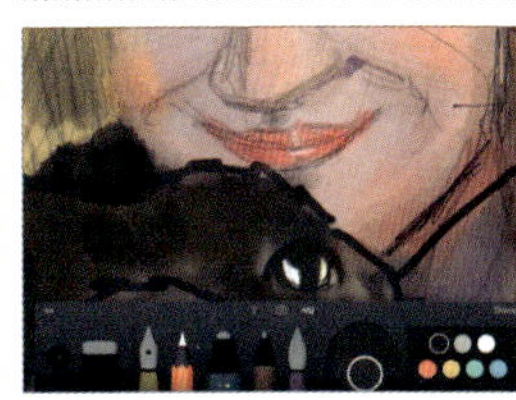

3 Put in ink
Select the pen and sketch over your painted area to add detail.

4 Fill in the blanks
Hold the eraser and select clear photo to check your progress.

News

Meet the iOS 9 replacement for Newsstand – your essential one-stop news digest on your iPad

You'll use it to...

Browse news sources
Pick the sources that matter to you

Read your digest
All the stories from all of your sources in one handy place

Share stories
Alert your friends to the top stories of the day

Save stories
Save the most gripping stories for later when you have time to enjoy them

Your one-stop for news

The News app, which will appear on your Home screen as part of the iOS 9 update, replaces the old Newsstand app (all of your previous digital publications will now be grouped together as separate apps in a 'Newsstand' folder elsewhere on your Home screen) and provides an essential digest for all of your favourite news sources. By accessing all of the news that matters most to you through one app, you're saving yourself the time it would take to access each source's respective app individually (Fig 1).

Setting up

When you first launch the News app you will be invited to pick one or more of your favourite news sources from an extensive selection to personalise the experience for you. These sources will provide the content for the app, but you can add more at any point or remove sources later on that you feel aren't doing the business. All of the content from the sources that you pick will appear in the 'For You' section of the app. As all of the content is updated regularly, you can swipe down while in the 'For You' view to

Fig 1 (above) The news from your preferred sources will be presented in your own personal feed. Swipe down to update it

Fig 2 (right) Tap on a previewed news story to read it all in its entirety in the fullness of your iPad's screen

refresh the content and update your feed with new stories as and when they become available.

When you see a story that you want to read, you can simply tap on it and you will be able to read it in its entirety using the full screen of your iPad (Fig 2). You can then tap the arrow to return to the main digest.

Your sources

To view your current preferred news sources, tap on the 'Favourites' section at the bottom of the interface and they will all be displayed onscreen. Tap on a source to only display the news from that particular source. For example, if you want to mine straight to the music news, tap on the NME source, or suchlike. You can also tap on the 'Edit' option in the top-right corner to remove certain sources from your collection if you find that you no longer read the news that they provide. Your news, your rules.

Explore new news

Like we mentioned earlier, you can add extra news sources to your feed that you didn't pick initially. To do this, tap on the 'Explore' section at the bottom of the interface and this will provide you with a range of suggested channels, suggested topics plus an extensive list of general categories that you can select to see even more sources that specialise in that field.

To add extra sources, simply tap on the '+' icon next to the respective source. Any sources listed that you have already included in your field will be marked by a tick icon.

Tap on the Search option to see a list of the current hot news topics that are currently trending

Setting up

1 Getting started
Launch the News app and then tap on the 'Get Started' option.

2 Pick your favourites
Scroll through the various news sources and select at least one.

3 Sign yourself up
With sources selected, tap 'Done' followed by 'Sign me up'.

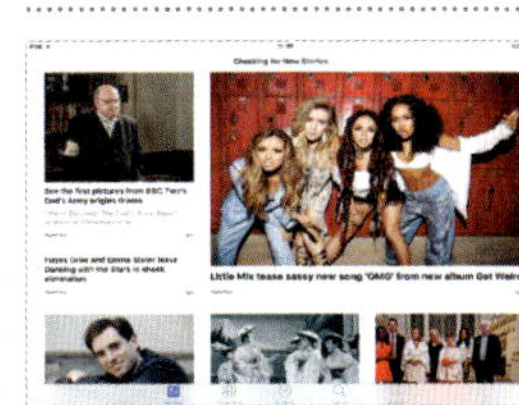

4 Your news digest
Based on your picks, the latest stories will be presented.

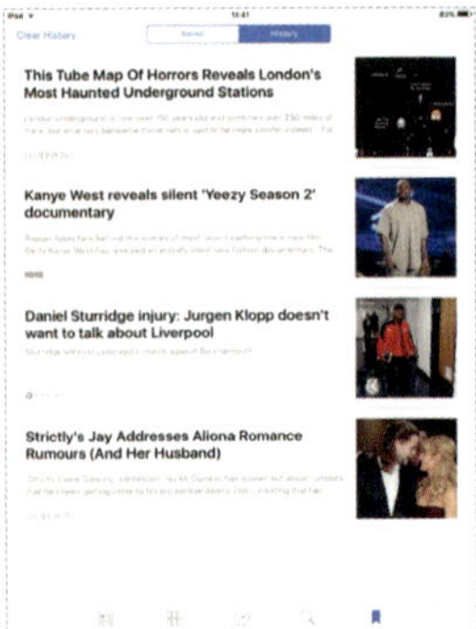

Fig 3 You can save stories to read later or find previously browsed content in History

Reading news stories

When you want to read the full content of a story that appears in your feed in the 'For You' section, tap on it to open it full screen. This will also present a selection of additional features. As always, you will see the share icon – tap this to share the current story through the usual array of sharing options, including your social networks. You will also see options here to open the story in Safari and add it to your Safari Reading List.

Tapping the heart icon will mark the story as a favourite, making it easy to pick out in the digest of stories. Better still, you can tap on the bookmark icon, which will save the story – this is particularly useful if you come across a story of interest but don't necessarily have the time to read it at the present time. Once a story has been

Share
You can share news stories through the usual variety of methods or even save them to your Safari Reading List

Your news
The News app tailors your feeds feed to meet your particular needs and requirements, so you only have to read the stories that are important to you

Save news
Tapping the bookmark icon will allow you to save a particular news story to the Saved section, making it easy to pick up where you left off when you have time to read

Mark stories
If you tap this heart icon then you will mark the story you're reading as a favourite, making it much easier to spot within the news feed

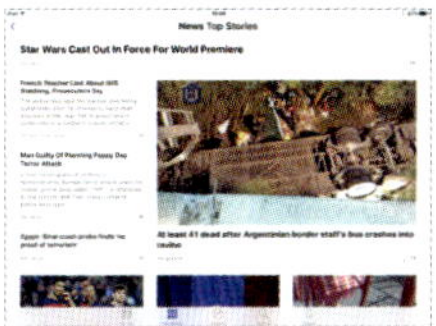

Subscribe to Apple's 'Top News' by making it one of your favourites to always stay in the know!

saved, you can then tap on the 'Saved' section at the bottom of the interface to take you to the list of your saved stories. This is useful as you don't risk losing the story in the avalanche of new content the is regularly refreshed into your feed.

The Saved section also includes a handy 'History' tab that you can tap on to see all of the stories that you have tapped on to read. So even if you forget to save a story, you can still find it with relative ease through this section (Fig 3).

Searching for news

The only other section within the News app that we haven't really touched on yet is the Search facility. When you tap on this you will initially be opresented with a list of all of the current hot news topics that are trending throughout the world. However, if none of those tickle your fancy then you can enter keywords into the search field to find what you're really looking for.

As you enter keywords you will be presented with top hits, that nail your desired topic head-on or secondary topics that feature one or more of the keywords you have entered. Simply tap on one of the topics to reveal the content.

Enable background app refresh

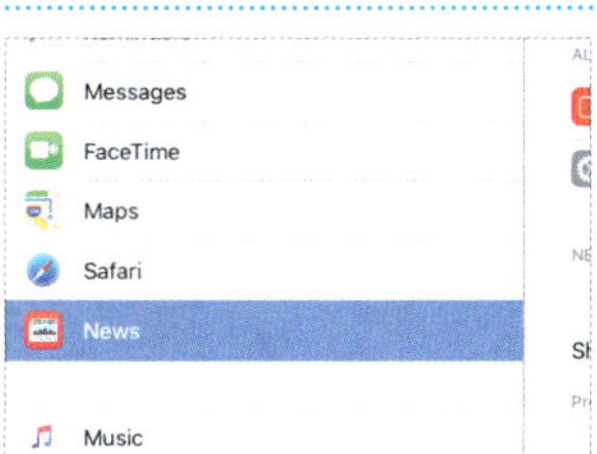

1 Go to Settings
Launch your Settings app and then go to the 'News' section.

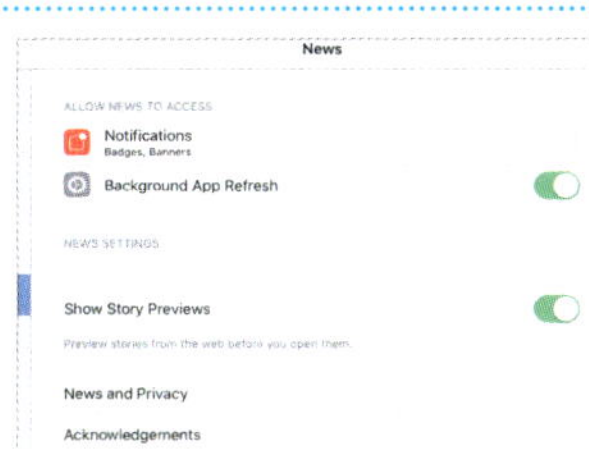

2 Enable the option
Enable the 'Background App Refresh' option to update content constantly.

Get News notifications

1 Go to the Settings
Navigate to the Settings app and tap on the 'News' section.

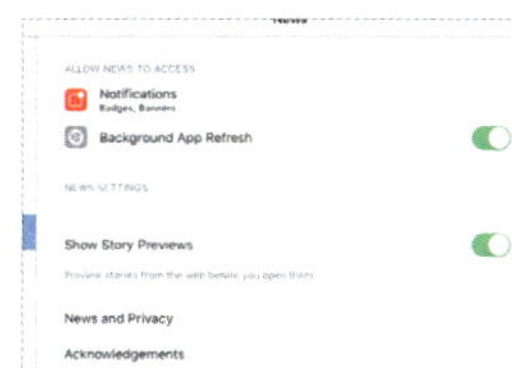

2 Tap on Notifications
Here you will see a section devoted to Notifications. Tap it.

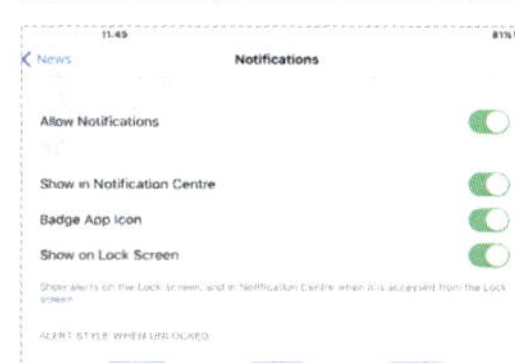

3 Allow notifications
Move the 'Allow Notifications' slider to the 'On' position.

4 Determine how
You can also choose the style of your News app notifications.

iBooks

Enjoy a good read without having to trek to the library, and save some trees at the same time

You'll use it to...

Buy books
Access the iBooks Store

Read fiction
Flick through thousands of novels

Scour textbooks
Educate yourself with learning materials

Save your PDFs
Place PDFs in iBooks

Search through books
Find specific terms within a text

Enlarge text
Make books comfortable to read

Read books on your iPad

Using iBooks, you can not only browse books and buy them in the iBooks Store, but you can also read them on your iPad and take advantage of great search facilities. The app puts an entire library of books at your fingertips (Fig 1).

The iBooks Store

The iBooks Store is the place to go to choose from thousands of books to buy and download to your iPad, both fiction and non-fiction. You can access the iBooks Store by going to the iBooks app, where you can choose either the Featured tab to view the latest books and deals, Top Charts to view the current best-sellers or Top Authors to search for books by author (Fig 2).

You can also search the store using the search facility in the top-right of the screen. If you have another iPad and you buy a book from the iBooks Store on it, you can have the book download to your iPad at no extra cost. Just go to the Purchased tab at the

Fig 1 (above) All of your downloaded books will be displayed in your library

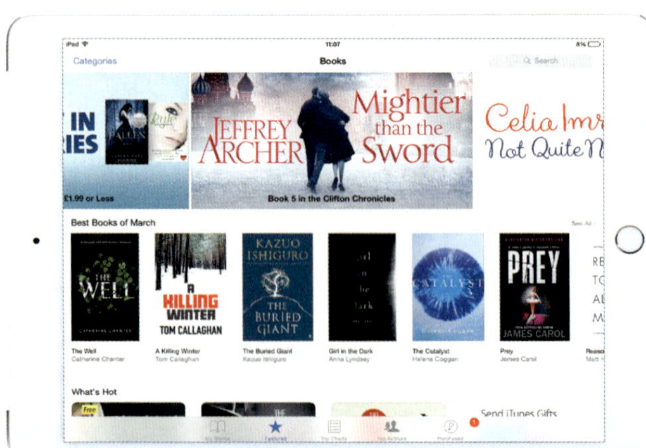

Fig 2 (right) The iBooks Store is packed with all kinds of books and you will be spoilt for choice

bottom of the screen to view all of your past purchases and tap on the 'Not on this iPad' section to view all of the books that you have bought in the past that aren't currently on your iPad.

Sample or buy a book

To buy a book, search for the one you want and then tap it. An information window will appear showing the book description, ratings, reviews and any related books. Standard book information is also shown.

As well as being able to share the information via Mail, Twitter and Facebook, you have two further choices: to sample the book or to buy it outright. Downloading a small sample will let you 'try before you buy', but if you tap the price to buy, your Apple ID or fingerprint will be requested before the whole book is downloaded to your iPad.

Navigate an ebook

When you are in your iBooks Library, simply tap on a book you want to read and it will open. By flicking your fingers left and right you are able to go back and forth between the pages. You will also see a scroll bar at the bottom of the screen. This lets you jump directly to a page, the number of which will be displayed below.

At the top of the screen, you will see more options. These include the ability to go back to your Library or select one of the book's chapters. You can adjust the text size, brightness of the screen, font style and themes such as Night mode or Scroll to suit your preferences. Tap on the magnifying glass icon and you can search for certain words and phrases but, handily, using the right-most icon, you can bookmark pages too.

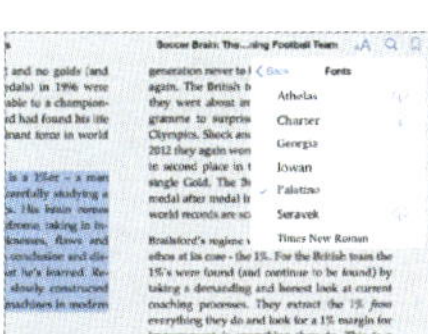

You can change the font of any book you read by tapping the font icon in the top-right

Activate Night mode

1 Find a book
Open a book you want to read at night and tap the font option.

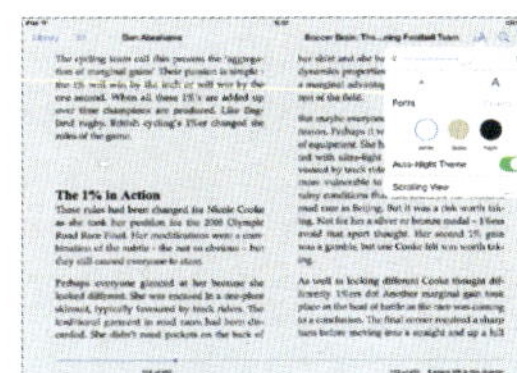

2 Select Theme
Select the Theme option on the box underneath the font button.

3 Select Night
Tap on Night and you will notice that the screen goes dark.

4 White on black
The effect is white text on black. To go back tap Normal.

iBooks

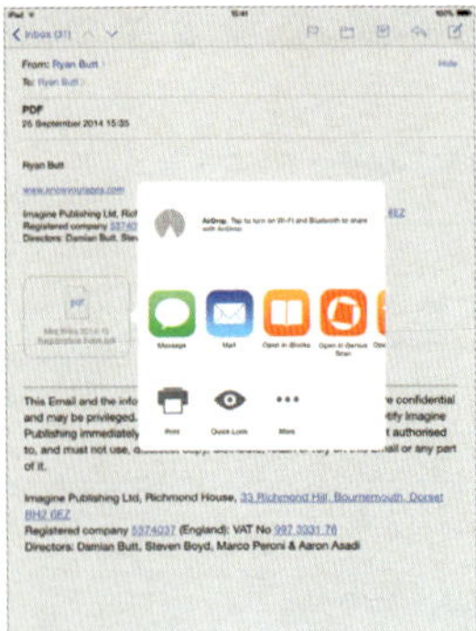

Fig 3 You can save and view PDFs and ePub attachments in iBooks

Read attachments from Mail

When you receive an email with a PDF or ePub attachment, it's possible to send it to iBooks for storage and to read. Simply tap on the PDF in the Mail app and it will open up for you to read through. Tap on the document to download it, and you will be presented with more options for what to do with the file (Fig 3). As well as being able to send it to someone via Mail or print it, you will also be able to open your PDF in iBooks. Tap on this option and the iBooks app will activate automatically.

Your PDF or ePub file will then be displayed in iBooks and become part of your iBooks library. This allows you to search through it, send it by email, print, produce notes and keep it safe for future reference.

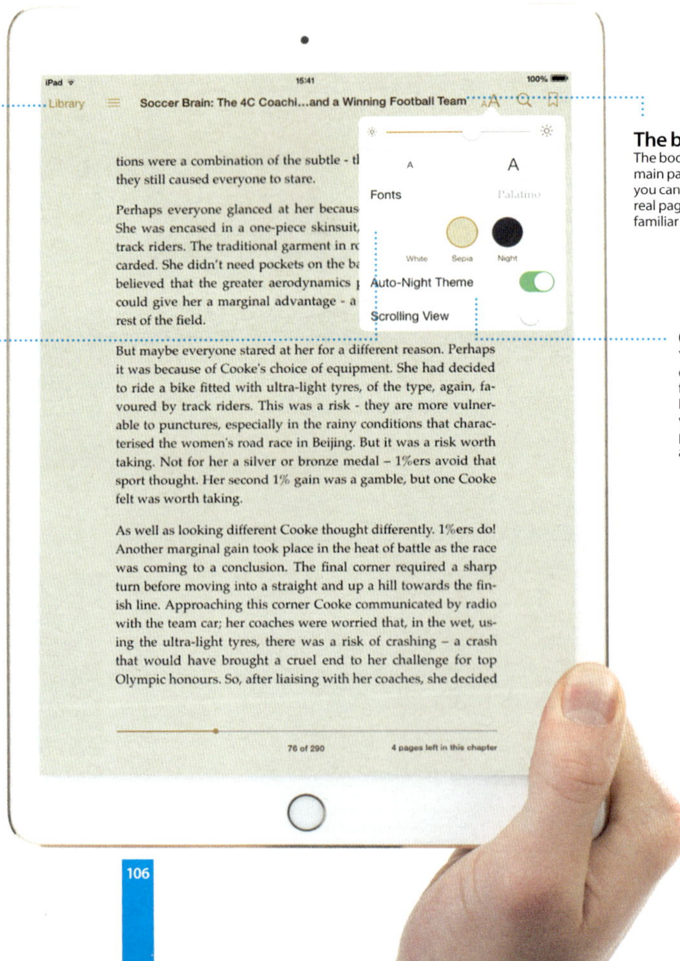

Library
At the top of the screen, you can go back to your library or, if you have a sample, buy the whole book to read

Themes
Normal is what you see here, Sepia adds a classic hue, and Night features white text on a black background

The book
The book appears in the main part of the screen. As you can see, it looks like a real page of a book with familiar formatting

Options bar
You can also change the font, search and bookmark. Night vision and full page modes are available too

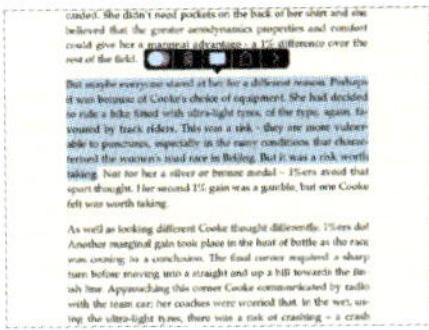

To remove a highlight, select the word or phrase and use the trash can icon to delete

To find PDFs in iBooks, tap on the Collections button at the top of the screen and select PDFs. A list of PDFs on your iPad will show together with a thumbnail of the file.

Annotate and make notes

You can annotate and make notes on an iBook. This is great if you are reading a textbook or educational paper, for instance, as you will be able to highlight certain parts of it and make references which will undoubtedly be a big help with your work and future revision. But even when you're reading for pleasure, whenever you need to have this facility it will be there.

Accessing it is easy and is simply a case of highlighting a word by pressing on it and then using the blue circles to expand the phrase. A selection of options appears on the screen and you can make your choice. Any notes and annotations you make are automatically saved to the book so that you can keep coming back to it for reference without worrying that they have disappeared.

As well as the ability to annotate and make notes, you can also search the text for identical words or phrases which may help you with further comments.

How to take notes

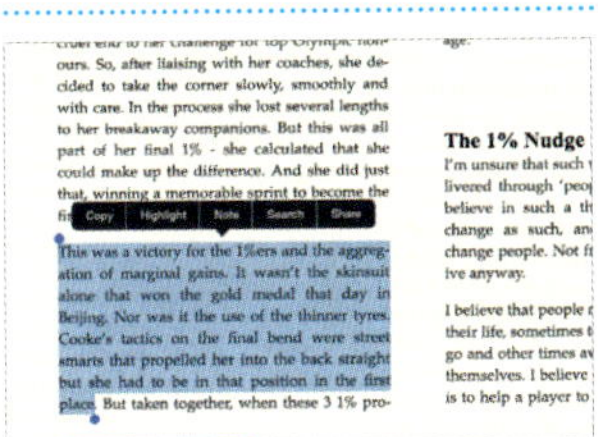

1 Select
Tap, hold and drag on a word or phrase. Then select Highlight or Note.

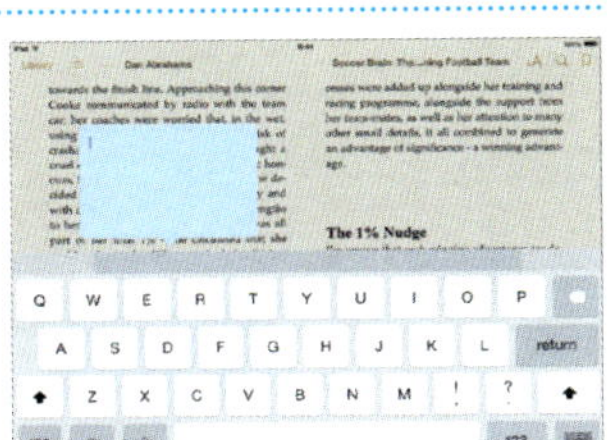

2 Make notes
Now use the keyboard to write a comment on your selected passage.

Add a bookmark

1 Find a page
To bookmark a page, first tap the icon in the top right.

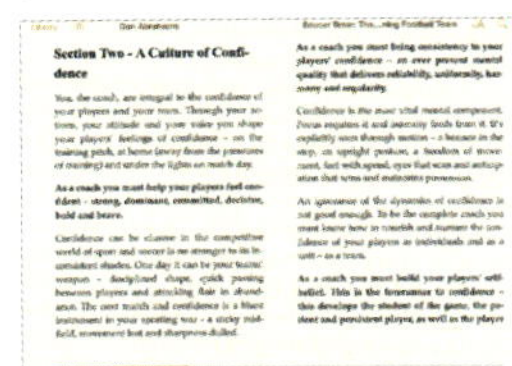

2 Red bookmark
A red bookmark symbol will mark your page and remain there.

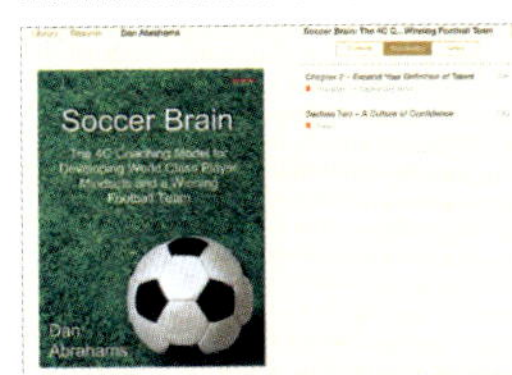

3 View bookmarks
To see bookmarks, tap the chapter button for a list.

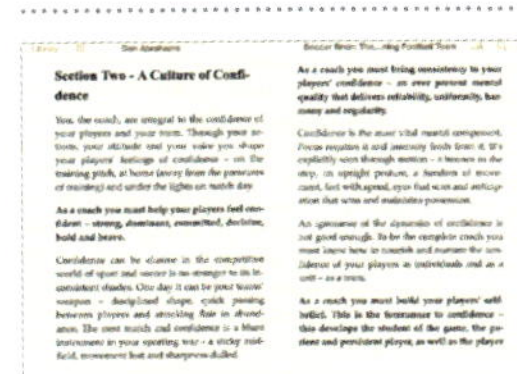

4 Remove bookmark
Tap on the red marker and the bookmark will disappear.

Game Center

Game Center is the place to be when playing games on your iPad

You'll use it to...

Track achievements
Use Game Center to view your in-game achievements

Add friends
Quickly add and link friends to your Game Center profile

Play turn-based games
Team up, take it in turns or go head-to-head with others

Manage challenges
Accept or decline challenges from friends

Find recommended games
Uncover new and exciting games to play

Connect with nearby players
Find nearby players over Wi-Fi/Bluetooth to play against

Play games with friends

Game Center is a useful portal for not only handling your in-game achievements, but also to instigate local/online multiplayer games. Additionally you can use it to manage any challenges you may have been sent, ie beat my score! Or keep an eye on global leaderboards to see where you're placed!

Set up Game Center profile

If you have an Apple ID (ie the one you use for setting up iCloud or iTunes) you are one step closer to setting up a Game Center Profile.

With iOS 9 you can sign in from either the Game Center App or via the Home Screen>Settings>Game Center option and then use the aforementioned Apple ID. Of course if you don't have an Apple ID the link will also be available to allow you to create one. Note: The settings method is also where you can logout of Game Center and log-in with a different profile, toggle Invites On/Off, setup friend recommendations or change your nickname if you make a mistake.

Fig 1 (above) Game Center is the main platform for managing your local/online games

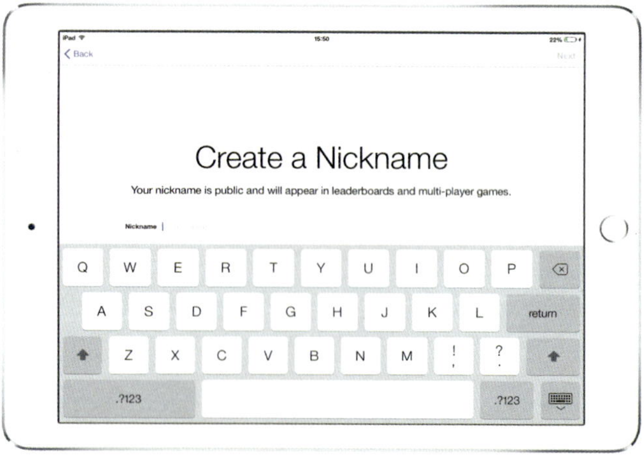

Fig 2 (right) All you need to set up a Game Center profile is your existing Apple ID

However in this example if you use the Game Center approach, you'll find that after signing in to the service you can then follow the wizard to setup your profile; this includes the aforementioned nickname (which allows others, ie your friends to locate you better) and the ability to add a photo/status message to give your profile more of a personal touch.

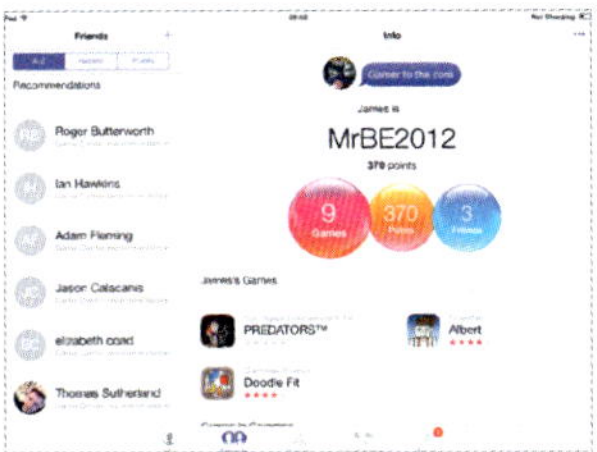

Find friends

Finding Friends on Game Center is not as difficult as you may think. For example during the initial setup wizard you may have been requested to link your Facebook/Contacts to your profile; if not you can enable this via the Home Screen>Settings>Game Center option (additionally you need to have setup iCloud Contacts and linked Facebook to your iOS account). Game Center then uses this information to recommend friends, which you can access via the 'Friends' tab to instigate a Friend Request.

Challenge others

The Game Center's local or multiplayer options (including competitive, coop or turned based games) are usually instigated from within a game's multiplayer menu. But you can participate in a less aggressive option called 'Challenges'. You can send 'Challenges' by first selecting a Game via the Games tab at the base of the screen and then under 'Achievements' tap the Achievement icon you want and when prompted choose 'Challenge Friends'. From here you can send a message to your mates to see if they can get the achievement. You can then monitor the responses or challenges you receive by using the 'Challenges' menu tab.

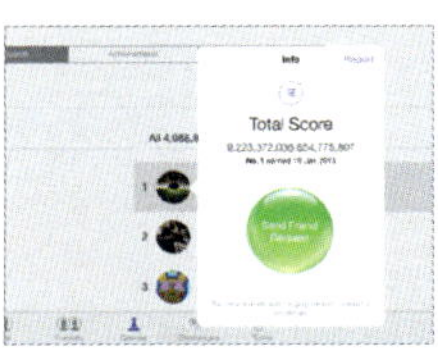

You can also send Friend Requests to players via the Games> Leaderboards section

Send a Friend Request

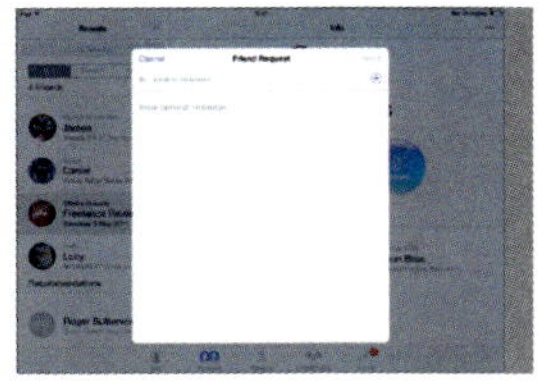

1 Add a friend
Select the 'Friends' tab at the base and then click the + sign.

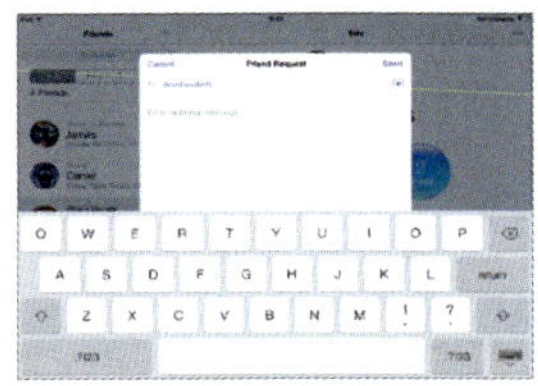

2 Key in details
Now key in their email address or their nickname.

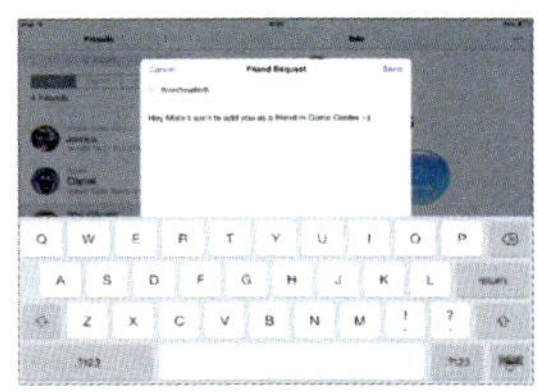

3 Send a request
You can now fill in a message and finish by selecting 'Send'.

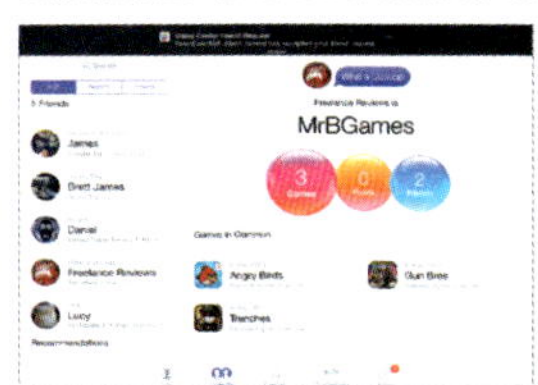

4 View your friends
If they accept your request they will appear under the 'Friends' tab.

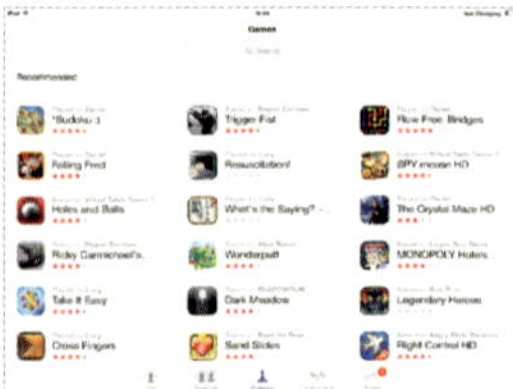

Fig 3 Game Center will automatically display a list of recommended Game Center-compatible games

Find new games

As we have mentioned, Game Center is pretty useful for keeping track of achievements and playing games with your friends. But the key ingredient here is to find games that are compatible with the platform in the first place. Back in the early days Game Center titles were not as common, so at times it felt like you were looking for a needle in a haystack. Thankfully the latest versions of the app are vastly improved, and finding new games has never been easier.

For example, launch Game Center and head to the 'Games' tab, your iPad will be scanned automatically and any compatible games are listed under the 'My iOS Games section'. Alternatively, at the top of the screen it will list a series of 'Recommended Titles' that can be expanded using the 'Show More' option. You can also head to the App Store and select any game and then view the 'Supports' information beneath the description. This tells you if the game is compatible or not. Alternatively, from the App Store, find the Featured tab and look for the 'Better with Game Center' option; this will also list compatible Game Center titles.

Leaderboards
The Leaderboards tab will allow you to see your rank against the rest of the world or your friends

Rate the game
Within the Games section you can also rate games, or if you have Facebook integration tap on 'Like'

Achievements
You can keep track of your Achievements and view what needs to be done to achieve them

Players
The Players tab can be used to view which of your friends also play the same game

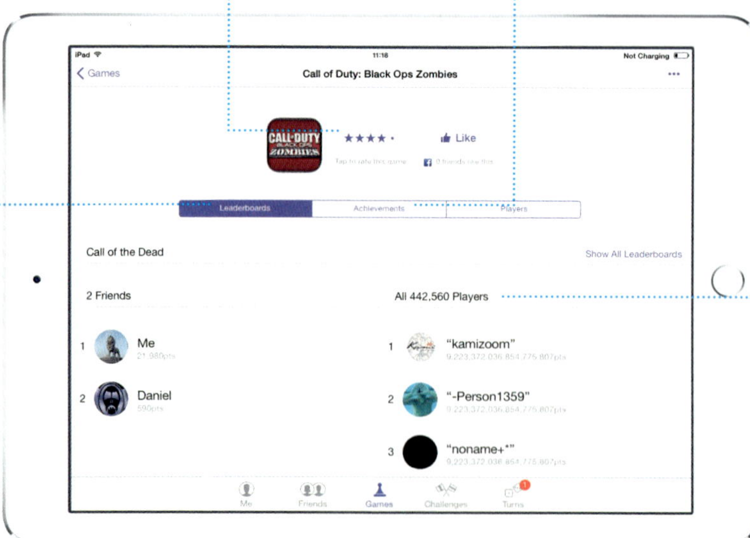

Nearby players can invite you to games over a Wi-Fi or Bluetooth connection if you turn the setting on

View Leaderboards and achievements

Achievements are purposely built into games to give you a purpose/goal, for example completing a certain task may unlock a special achievement and this should then give you the drive to get more out of the game. With the iOS 8 platform you can use the 'Games' tab to view all of your currently listed titles and the achievements they hold.

With Achievements these are split into two parts, the ones you have earned, which are symbolised by a graphical icon, or the ones that aren't, which are listed with a question mark inside. Additionally each achievement will provide a small description to give you the heads up as to how you can unlock it.

In certain games, you may also notice the Leaderboards tab at the top. This will display how many points you have earned within a game compared to the rest of the world, and see if you are currently ahead of your friends. It's worth nothing that you can switch between Leaderboards using the 'Show All Leaderboards' option.

At this stage you can also share your points/achievements with others (or gloat to your beaten friends in other words). It's this process we cover next in a small tutorial below.

Share your points total

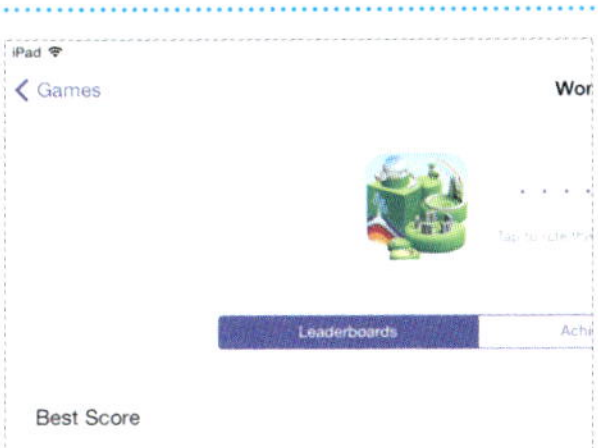

1 Select a friend
Under the Leaderboards tab within a game, select yourself.

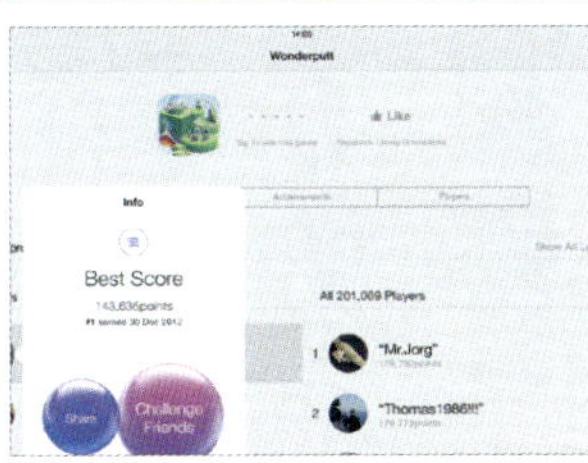

2 Share results
Tap on the 'Share' option and choose how you want to share, ie 'Twitter'.

Take your turn

1 Search for games
Within the App Store install 'Naval Warfare', for example.

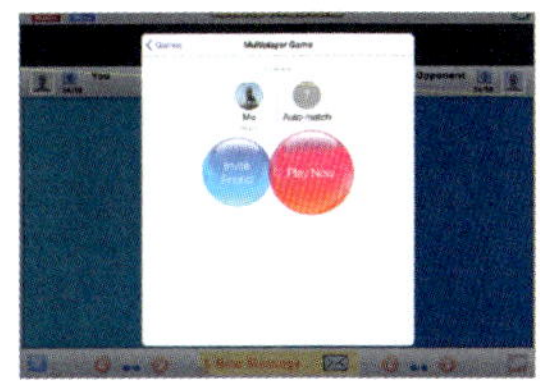

2 Set up friends
Within the main game invite a friend to your game.

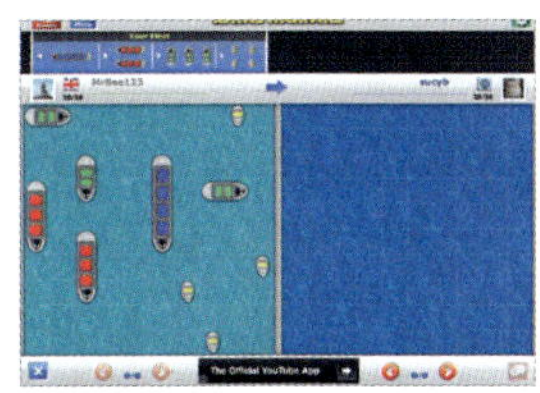

3 Monitor your turn
Play your move and head to Game Center to monitor moves.

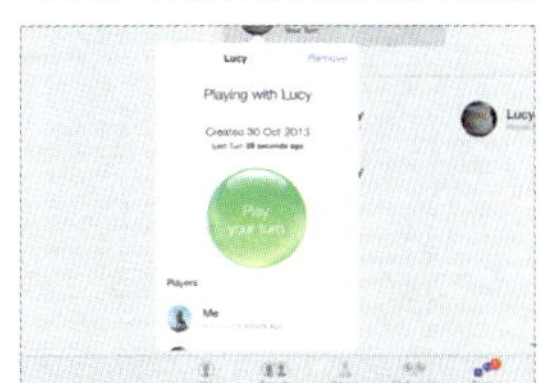

4 Take a turn
Under 'Turns' tap the game and when choose 'Play your turn'.

iCloud Drive

The easy way to store all of your presentations, spreadsheets, PDFs, images and other documents and access them anywhere

You'll use it to…

Back up files
Keep all of your prized documents safely stored in one place

Transfer files
Open files in other apps beyond the native ones that created them

Shift files between devices
Moves files between devices with iOS 8 or 9 and Macs running Yosemite or El Capitan

Work remotely
Continue working on your office presentation while you commute

Collaborate
Share and collaborate on documents with your work colleagues

Save instantly
Any changes you make to documents will be reflected on all devices

Freedom to work

What the iCloud Drive brings to the iPad is a robust and reliable cloud storage service that enables you to store all of your documents, presentations, spreadsheets, PDFs, images and more, and access them anywhere in the world whenever you need them from your iPhone, iPad, iPod touch, Mac or PC. It's very much like other cloud computing services such as Dropbox and Google Drive, but it's built into the very fabric of your device's operating system, which means it is incredibly easy to use. To get started using the service, open the Settings app, select the iCloud section and scroll down the list of enabled services. Tap on iCloud Drive and then choose the 'Upgrade to iCloud Drive' option (Fig 1).

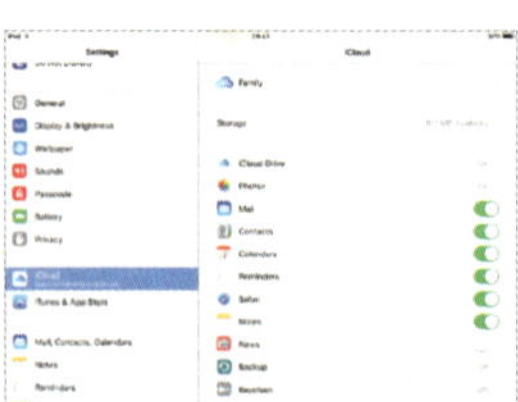

Fig 1 (above) When you choose to upgrade to iCloud Drive the process may take a few minutes

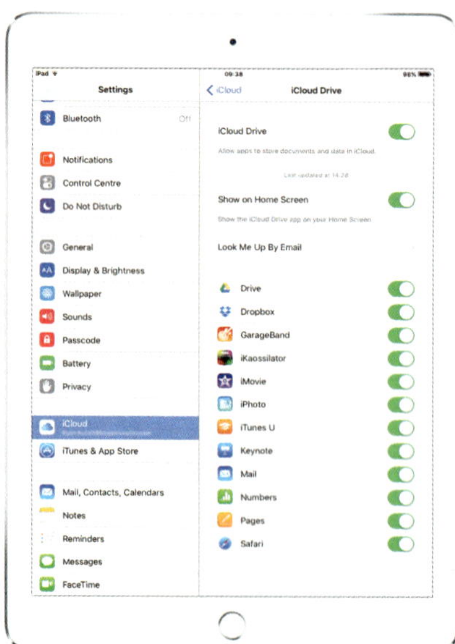

Fig 2 (right) Go to your iCloud Drive Settings to enable apps to use the service

Transferring files

To upload files to iCloud, simply drag them into the iCloud Drive on your Mac (running OS X El Capitan) or PC (running Windows 7 or later) or create a new document using an iCloud-enabled app on your iPad (such as the Pages, Numbers or Keynote apps) which will be auto-uploaded to your iCloud account and retrievable on the other systems mentioned above. Using iCloud means that you'll always have access to the latest version of all your documents from any device because all changes are synced automatically. So if you start creating a document on your Mac at work, you can make the final edits at home later on your iPad – and all of the changes you make will be automatically saved and reflected on all of your devices. To enable apps, launch your Settings app, tap on 'iCloud', then 'iCloud Drive' and move the app sliders to On (Fig 2).

Transferring files

With iCloud Drive, all of your files are made accessible outside the confines of the app that created them. So when you tap to open a file on your iPad and choose your iCloud Drive account as your source, instead of just seeing the files associated with the app in question, you will see a document picker with folders representing all of the apps on your device (in theory anyway, the provision is that the developers of the respective apps must make these folders public, which should be done via regular software updates – so check the App Store to see if the app whose files you wish to access has an update pending). Tap on one of the folders and you willl see the files contained in that app. Tap on one of those files and you will be able to import the file into the app, within reason.

Once you have access to an external file, that file will remain accessible to the current app and to you. As well as opening files, iCloud Drive can also be used to import them instead. For example, if you wanted to bring slides from one Keynote presentation into another, the file with the additional slides could be imported instead of opened.

You can view your iCloud Drive as a list by swiping down and then tapping the icon in the top-right

Enable the iCloud Drive app in iOS 9

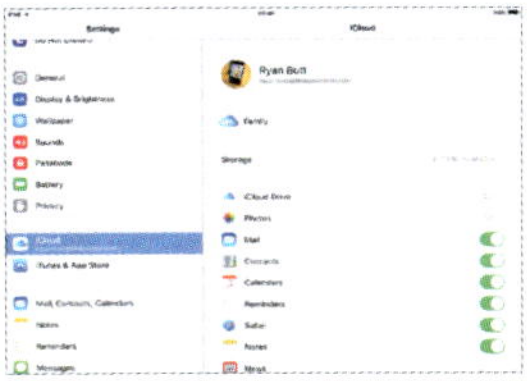

1 Go to Settings
In the Settings app, select iCloud, then tap on iCloud Drive.

2 Show on Home screen
Enable the 'Show on Home Screen' option.

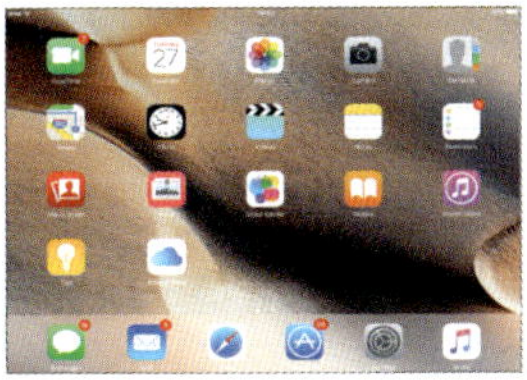

3 Access your Drive
Your iCloud Drive will now appear as an app on your Home screen.

4 Organise your Drive
You can now view, organise and manage your iCloud Drive files.

iMovie

Create movies and trailers using iMovie's superb range of editing facilities

You'll use it to...

Create movies
Build a great movie by adding videos, photos and audio

Make trailers
Hollywood-style film trailers can be made from simple templates

Apply themes
Select a theme and customise how the finished video will look

Apply special effects
Insert transitions between video clips and customise them

Precision editing
Learn how to edit the clips and audio with a fine degree of control

Export movies
Save movie projects to the Camera Roll or share them online

Fig 1 (above) Ready-made video project templates make it easy to produce high-quality movies

Fig 2 (right) Detach an audio track from a video, add another and then fade it in

Create and edit films

Making movies has never been so easy and iMovie is a fantastic app that makes the process lots of fun. It enables you to browse and select the videos that you wish to include, add photos and music, and then it outputs a movie that looks like it was professionally made.

Features in iOS 9

iMovie is as intuitive as the rest of iOS 9, but that isn't all there is to this great app. Among the features is an excellent video browser. Select Videos at the top to see film strips showing all the clips on your iPad. Tap one and a larger video window appears with tortoise and hare icons on the left. Tapping these plays the video at half or double speed, which is really useful. A heart button enables you to add it to your favourites. The Share button enables you to share video clips through social networking sites and via Mail and Messages right from the browser.

There are great audio capabilities, such as the ability to detach audio from the video in the timeline, trim, split and reposition music and sound effects, and adjustable audio fade-in and fade-out. Tap a video clip, select Audio at the bottom and use Detach and Fade.

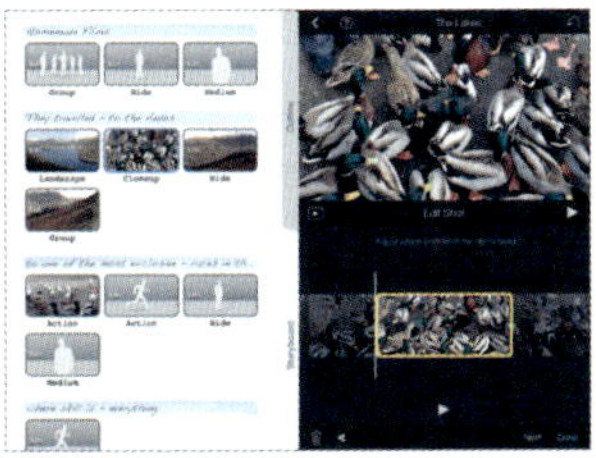

Make a movie with trailers

Select Projects at the top, tap the plus and you have a choice of creating a movie or trailer. The latter is a different way to show off your movies and it creates one that looks like a Hollywood trailer. You add the best scenes from your videos, enter the titles and captions, and it builds the trailer from them. Press play under a trailer to preview it.

Add titles and transitions

Transitions between scenes can give your movie a unique look and are fun to use. Create a movie project, tap Videos at the top and add two clips. Where one changes to another is a gap with an icon in the middle. Press it and at the bottom are transition buttons. Tap one then press the time on the right to set the duration. To add a title to a clip, tap it in the timeline, press Title at the bottom and choose Opening, Middle or Closing to set the position, then enter the text to be displayed.

Use iMovie themes

To make video editing easier and to help you create professional-looking results, iMovie includes a collection of top-quality themes to get you started. They consist of a collection of co-ordinated screen

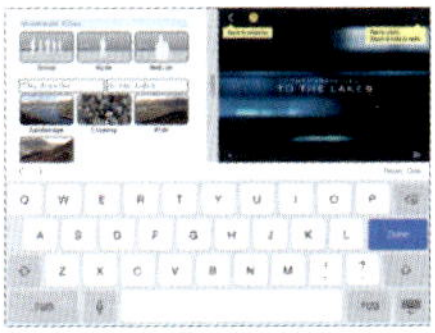

When creating a trailer, you need to tap the text in the storyboard to edit titles

Import footage

1 Shoot it
Create a new project and tap the camera button to shoot video.

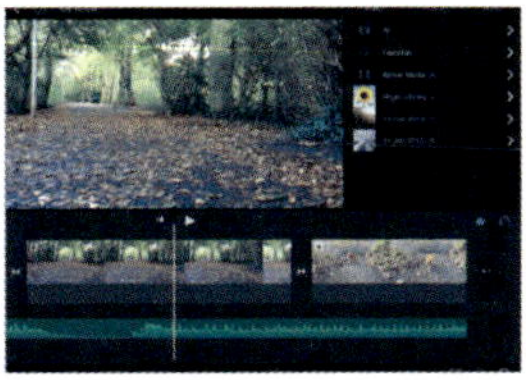

2 Video libraries
Press Video and different sources of video clips are displayed.

3 Import clips
Select one of the videos and tap the down arrow.

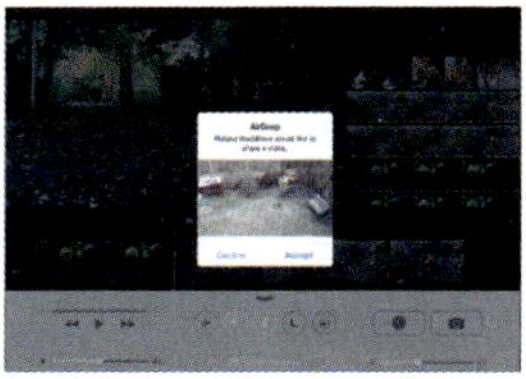

4 Use AirDrop
Pull up Control Centre and enable AirDrop, then send a video.

Fig 3 The theme you choose determines how titles and transitions as shown

titles, a set of transitions, and matching music that all fits together neatly. Go to the Projects screen and tap the plus button to create a new one, then select the Movie option rather than Trailers. Theme thumbnails are displayed at the bottom and you can swipe left and right to browse them. A large image of the currently selected theme is displayed and the play button below can be used to preview what the theme will look like.

Choose the Simple theme, Playful, Neon or whatever is appropriate. Don't worry too much about which theme you choose, as you can quickly change it from within the project at any time. On the edit screen, press the settings button in the bottom-right corner to display the themes panel and then select a different thumbnail. You can also customise various other options, such as whether to

Recording
Press the camera or microphone icons to input video or audio directly into the project editor

Titles
Tap a video to select it and press Titles to add text. The T icon indicates this clip has titles

Libraries
Select Video, Photos or Audio to browse for items to add to the video project timeline

Settings
Tap this icon to view the theme panel. Change themes, turn music on or off and more

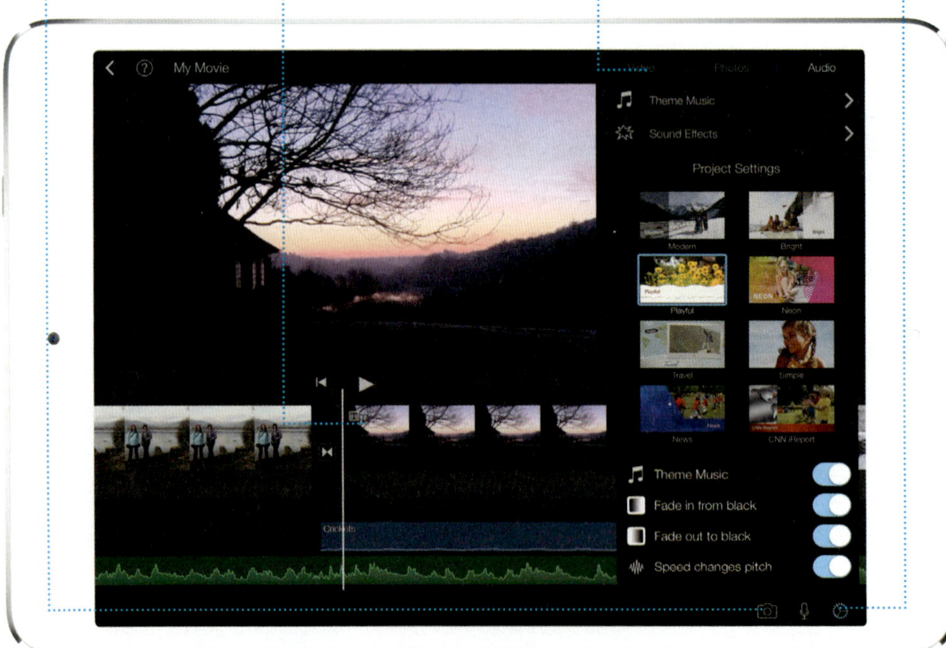

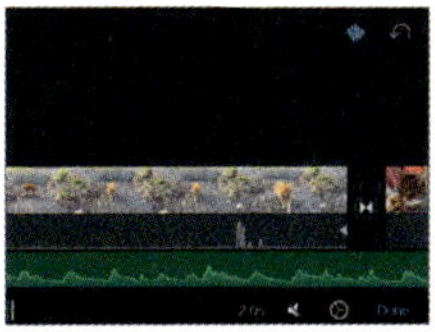

If you can't see the audio track, tap on the audio button, represented by a wiggly line icon

have theme music, and whether the movie should fade in or out from black.

Precision Editor

After adding two or more videos to the timeline at the bottom of the screen, there are two tasks you might want to perform. One is to trim the start and end of a video clip and the other is to set exactly how they are to transition from one to the other. For this you need the Precision Editor. Select a video clip in the timeline and there are yellow bars at each end. Press and drag these bars to adjust the point at which a clip starts and the point it ends at.

Press the icon between two video clips to display the transitions options and a double-headed arrow appears. Tap this to use the Precision Editor. The two clips are displayed one on top of the other. Drag the yellow bars to choose where to end and start the transition from one clip to another. There is also a blue bar on the outgoing clip and this enables you to adjust when the sound cuts off. A common video-editing technique is to switch to the next scene's audio before the video and this is what it's for. When you've finished making the fine adjustments, press Done.

Edit clips

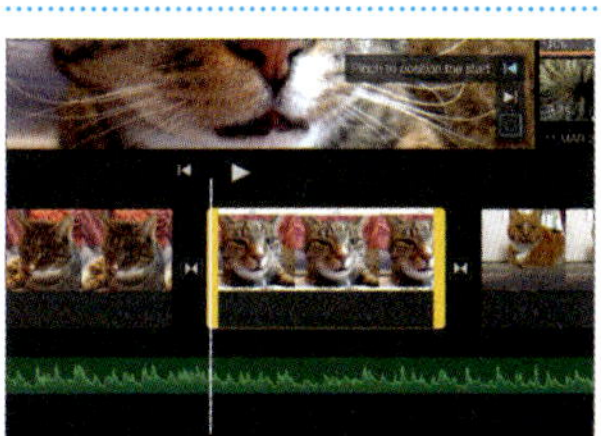

1 Trim it
Tap a video and drag the yellow bars to adjust the start/end.

2 Transition details
Tap a transition, then the arrow to make fine start/end adjustments.

Export your movie

1 The project
Select a project or go to Theatre, wherever there's a Share button.

2 Save video
These are many ways to export a video project. Press Save Video.

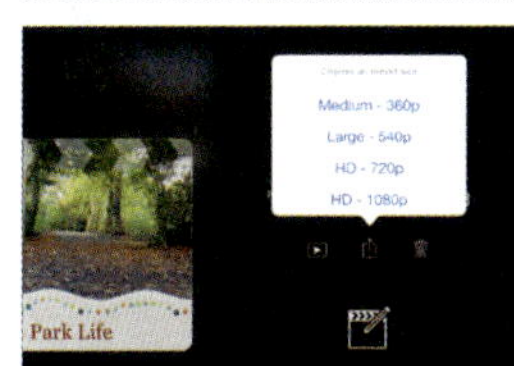

3 Resolution options
Select an export resolution and then save to Camera Roll.

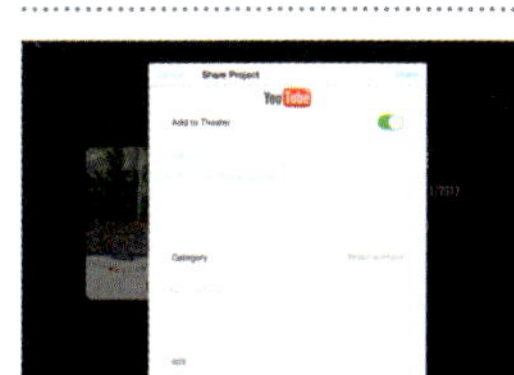

4 Export online
Select an option such as YouTube to export online.

GarageBand

GarageBand is a recording studio in your pocket with the ability to recreate instruments perfectly

You'll use it to...

Remember new tunes
If you suddenly think of a new tune or chord you can capture it immediately

Play new instruments
Play any instrument from a vast number of offerings

Use your own equipment
Attach your own instruments to play and record them instantly

Keep in sync
A great way to manage your songs automatically using iCloud

Mix and match
Mix many instruments and sounds into one multilayered song

Jam with friends
Play along with friends using wireless connections and make music together

Music made easy

GarageBand is capable of acting as a mini recording studio for all of your instruments. You can play many of the included instruments on the app or simply plug your own in for added realism. It comes standard as a native app on new iPads.

Create a song

Creating a song in GarageBand is as simple as doing so with real musical instruments. The interface is obvious enough to let anyone jump in and start straight away (Fig 1).

Begin by choosing an instrument from the many that are available via the Instruments icon in the top bar. Once you have decided what it is that you want to make music with, tap the red Record button at the top and simply start playing. You will hear a metronome in the background to help you keep time, and as soon as you are satisfied with what you've recorded you can press Stop at the top.

Fig 1 (above) GarageBand can help you achieve all of your musical aspirations with ease

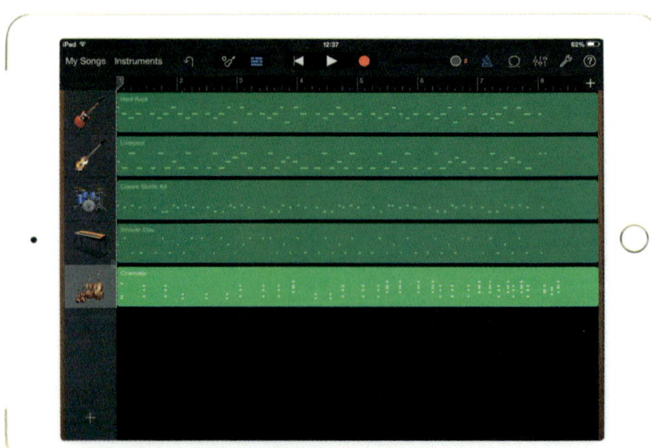

Fig 2 (right) You can layer several instrument tracks together to create a musical masterpiece

You can now play your track back to hear what it sounds like. It will be saved automatically, so you needn't worry about losing any of your musical masterpieces, and you can add further tracks (Fig 2).

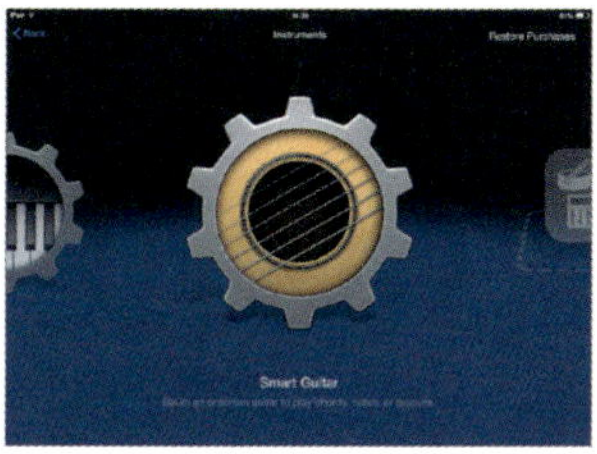

Use Smart instruments

Smart instruments take the notion of music creation to a whole new level for those who do not have much experience when it comes to instruments and other musical things. They are designed to let you create pitch-perfect music simply by playing around. However, they also offer some educational bonuses to help you understand chords and the way music is put together.

Go to Instruments and swipe across until you see the Smart Strings, Smart Drums, Smart Guitar, Smart Bass and Smart Keyboard. Select one of the instruments, for example Guitar, and the standard instrument panel will fill the screen. You will notice that chord names are shown above the strings – simply tap one of the names and the chord will play as if you strummed it perfectly.

You can also tap each string in order to understand how the chord is made up. Tapping the Autoplay button at the top will let you automatically adjust the speed at which chords are played to add extra variety.

Start a Jam Session

Jam sessions are invaluable to real bands, and GarageBand fully caters for the interaction required when practising or laying down new tunes. The Jam Session feature is available by tapping the tool icon to enable multiple devices to hook up via Bluetooth so everyone has creative input in composing new songs.

Choose Sampler from instruments to record a sound that will be played by the keyboard

Edit a track

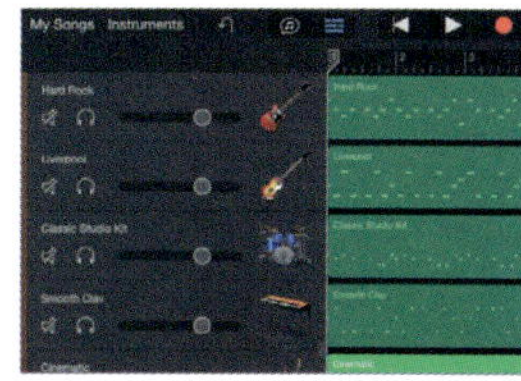

1 Tap and select a track
Tap on any track in Arrangement view to select it for editing.

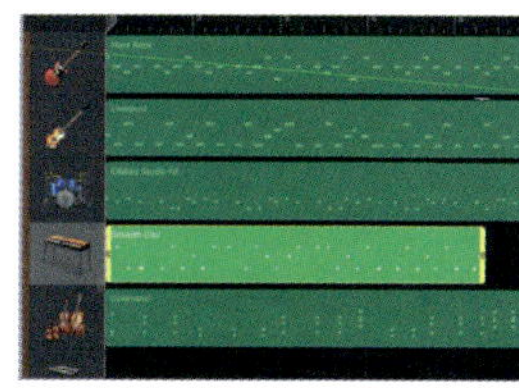

2 Drag and trim it
Drag the handles at either end of the track to trim the start or end.

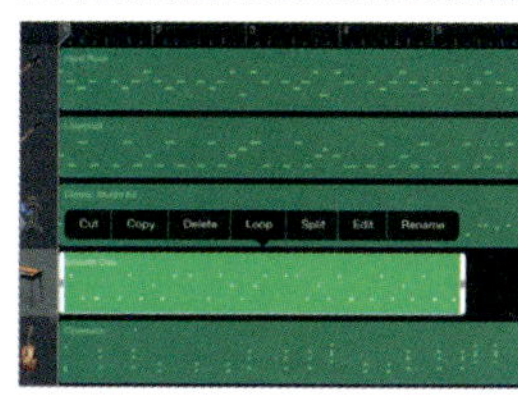

3 Extra options
Double-tapping a track will show extra options such as Cut or Split.

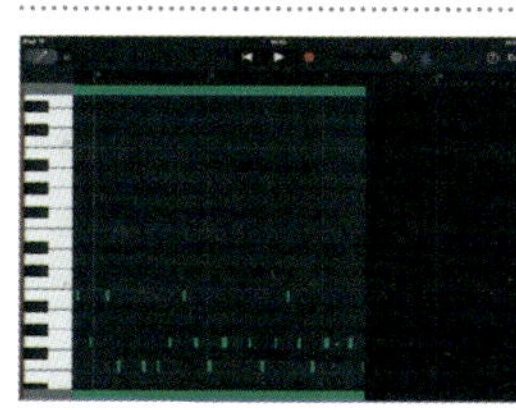

4 Open the piano roll editor
From these, tap Edit to open the advanced piano roll editor.

Pages

Create beautiful documents using Pages and share them with friends or work colleagues

You'll use it to...

Enter text
Use this great word processor for perfect letters, CVs and more

Embed photos
Insert photos to illustrate documents, add charts and other objects

Use templates
Select a ready-made template and you won't be worrying about design

Share documents
Choose how to share documents – as files or online using links

Export documents
Use the excellent export facilities – write a book and read it in iBooks

Use AirDrop
Send the finished documents to nearby people using AirDrop

A portable word processor

Pages is a great word processor at heart and whether you want to write a letter, report or book, you'll find the app is perfect for the task. It features spell checking on the fly so you can instantly see misspelt words, plus documents are auto-saved.

Features of Pages

Creating attractive and professional-looking documents in the Pages app is easy. There are lots of fantastic templates that you can use as a starting point for your own documents and you just replace the text and images with your own. A formatting toolbar just above the keyboard puts all your most-used controls just where you need them and formatting text is easier than ever.

Comments can be stored within documents and this is especially useful if you use the updated iCloud facilities. Share a link to a Pages document with someone and they can view and edit it with you. This is great for collaborating on documents and reports with

Fig 1 (above) Word processing in Pages is straightforward and it has lots of very useful features

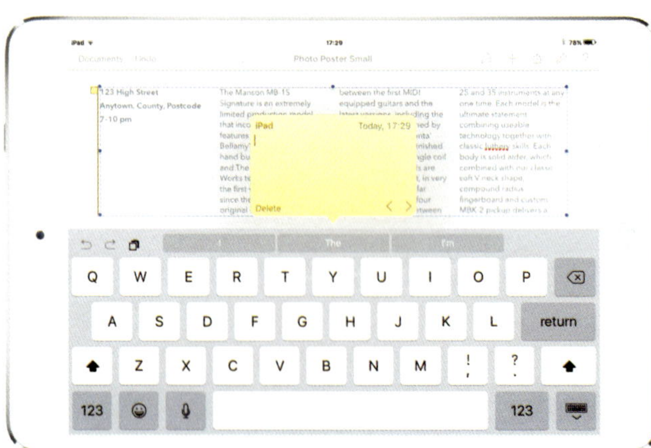

Fig 2 (right) Pages has a clean design and features like comments

friends or work colleagues. Pages isn't just for plain text, and charts can easily be inserted and there are now a number of animated ones that make documents interactive. There are excellent sharing facilities too.

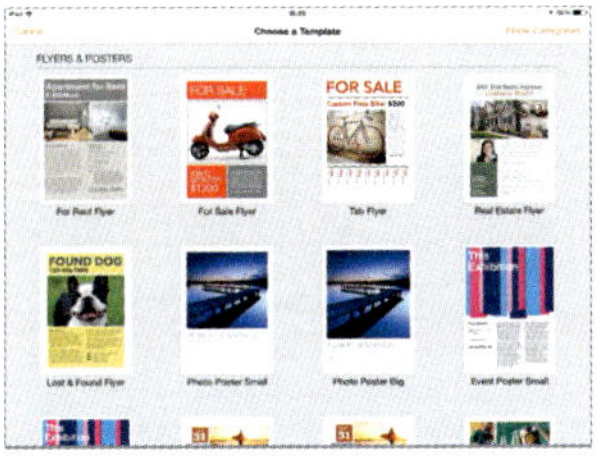

Create documents and work with templates

There are dozens of superb templates to choose from when you want to create a new document, and they are organised into categories like reports, letters, flyers and posters, newsletters and so on. From the home screen, press the plus button and select Create Document to see them. Select a template and when it opens, just replace the text and images with your own.

Use with AirPrint

Printing from Pages on your iPad is straightforward providing you have the right printer. If you have a model that supports Apple AirPrint, and an increasing number do these days, you can print any document with just a few taps. Open a document and press the Tools button in the top-right corner. Make sure the printer is switched on and then select Print. If it says Select Printer, press it and your iPad searches the Wi-Fi network for devices. You can then select it. Set the number of copies to print and then hit Print.

Work with images

Pages isn't just for dull and lifeless text; you can bring excitement to a dry subject by simply inserting some relevant, and interesting, images. They make a world of difference and they help to maintain

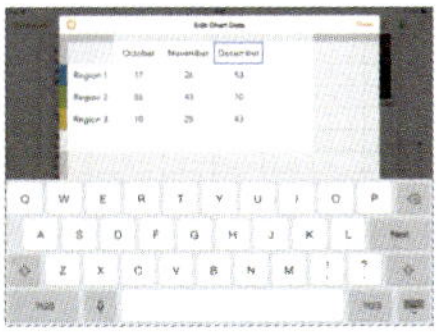

If you add an interactive chart, press it to edit the dummy data that's currently used

Find and replace

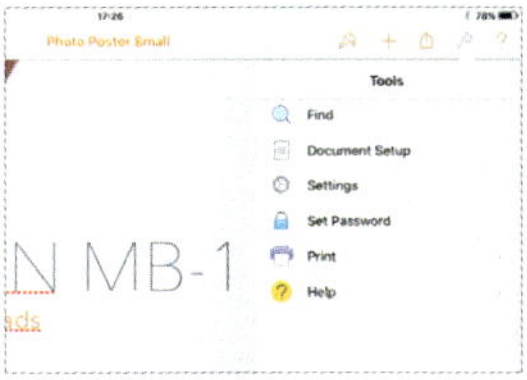

1 Tools menu
Tap the Tools icon and select Find on the menu that drops down.

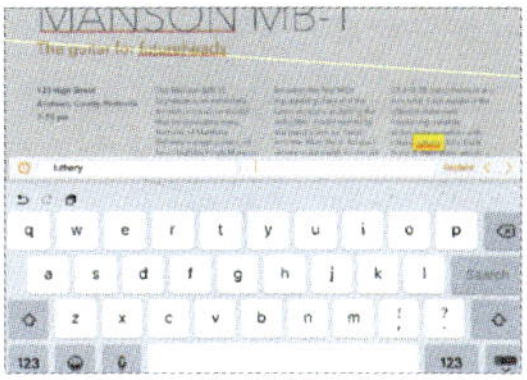

2 Find it
To Find text, just enter it into the search box above the keyboard.

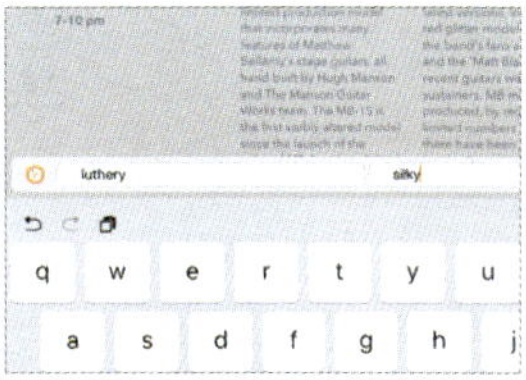

3 Locate text
All possible matches will be highlighted within the text.

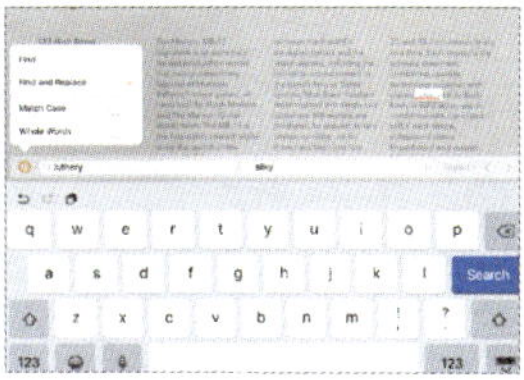

4 Replace it
Fill in the boxes and select the Replace option.

Fig 3 Use the menu at the top to insert objects like photos into documents

the reader's interest as well as illustrating points in the text. There are two ways of working with images and it depends on whether you are starting with a template or with a blank sheet of paper. Some templates – such as newsletters, flyers and posters – already contain images. These are just placeholders and the idea is that you replace them with your own images. Press the plus button in the bottom-right corner to replace the image with one from your Camera Roll.

If you start with a blank sheet, or if you want to add more images to a template, press the plus button at the top of the screen and select the first tab icon, which enables you to select photos from an album such as Camera Roll or your Photo Stream. The image is inserted, but it is rarely in the right place or is the right size. Press

Special items
When editing body text, tap this to insert a comment, page or column break, or to add a footnote

Format menu
The contents of the format menu reflects the object selected and is different for text, images and so on

Insert objects
This button is used to insert photos, tables, charts, text boxes, lines, arrows, curves and ready-made shapes

Tools
There are lots of options here, including password protection, tracking changes and document setup, such as margins

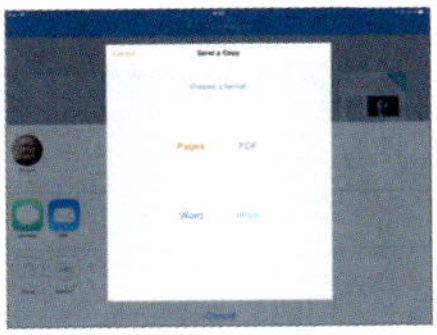

When Wi-Fi and Bluetooth are turned on, send the document to people via AirDrop

and drag the corners to resize it and press and drag the photo to position it on the page.

Share your documents

Documents created with Pages are not stuck on your iPad and they can easily be shared to your other devices, or with your friends or work colleagues. They don't need to have the same device as you, they can use an iPad, iPhone, iPod touch, Mac or Windows PC to view your Pages document. It is even possible to share a document using the iCloud website and allow anyone with a web browser to view it and edit it.

There are two ways to share a Pages document and one is by sending a copy of the whole file to someone. It can be sent as an attachment to an email message using Mail or an instant message in the Message app. AirDrop can also be used to send a file to someone, for example, a person nearby using an Apple Mac, iPad or iPhone on the same network. The other way to share a document is to provide a link to its location on iCloud. This link can then be posted in a message, an email, on social networking websites like Facebook and Twitter and so on.

Share documents on Facebook

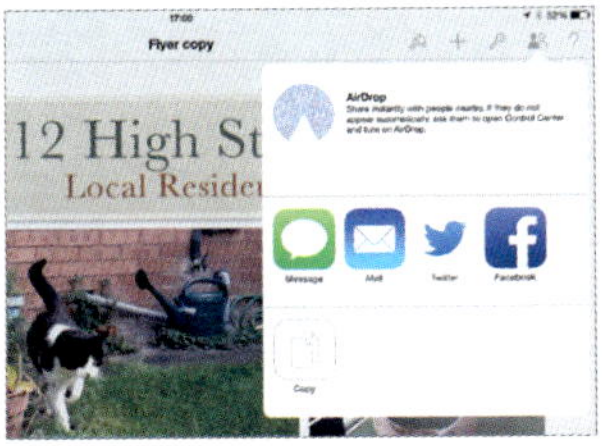

1 Choose a service
Press the Share button, select Share Link via iCloud and tap Facebook.

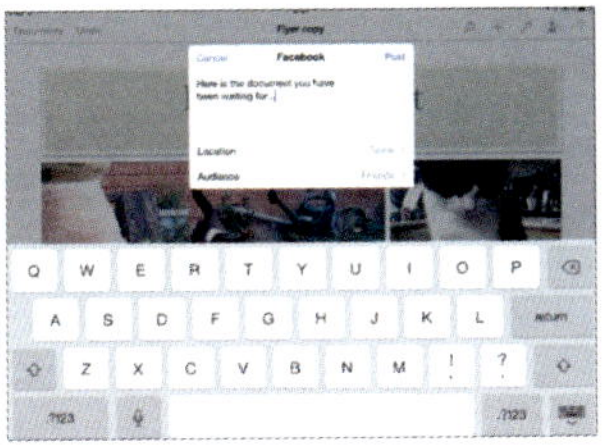

2 Add comments
The standard Facebook sharing form appears and you can add a comment.

Export documents

1 Sharing options
Open a document and tap Share. Tap 'Open in Another App'.

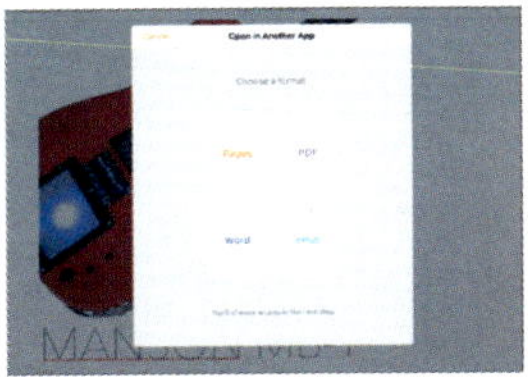

2 Format options
Four different file formats are available. Chose ePub.

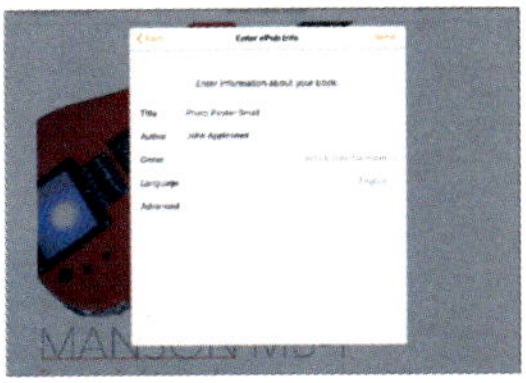

3 Additional information
Different options are presented for formats. Enter what's required.

4 Export options
As we've exported to ePub, there is an option to open it in iBooks.

Numbers

Build spreadsheets for fun, a hobby or for work using Numbers on your iPad

You'll use it to...

Create spreadsheets
Enter numbers and text to create a working spreadsheet

Use tables
Store numeric and financial information in tables

Use templates
Use ready-made spreadsheets for a wide range of purposes

Insert functions
Perform calculations on table data by inserting functions

Export spreadsheets
Convert spreadsheets into different file formats for exporting

Share them
Store your spreadsheets on iCloud and share links with others

Fig 1 (above) Numbers is designed to help you with financial planning and more

Fig 2 (right) A collection of attractive and easy-to-use templates are bundled with Numbers

Present figures in style

If you thought spreadsheets were just for company accounts, think again because Numbers is a great app with a wide range of uses for homes, hobbies and education. It stores numeric and financial information, analyses it and presents it in clear and striking ways.

Features in iOS 9

Numbers has a look that is cleaner and simpler than previous versions. It follows iOS 9's design theme and is attractive and easy to use, yet remains a powerful tool for analysing numeric and financial data. Among the features is a collection of templates and there are 30 of them. They cover a wide range of uses, from the handy personal budget, savings and loan spreadsheets to company invoices, employee schedules and so on. There are fun templates too, like a running log, party and travel planners.

Numbers has new interactive charts that enable you to see different information by clicking easy-to-use buttons and controls.

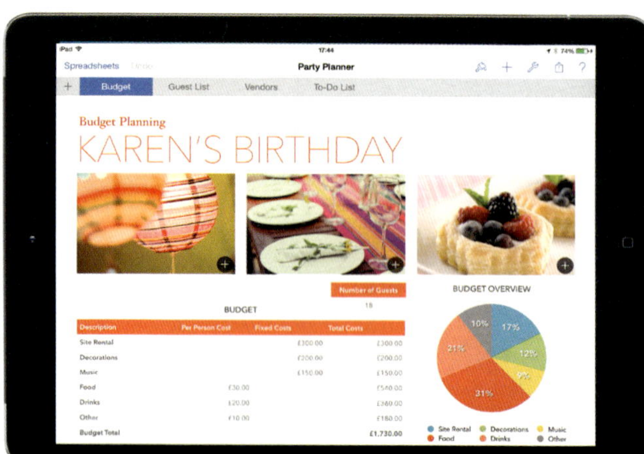

iCloud integration has been improved and a common file format means that you can create and edit the same document on an iPad, iPhone, Mac or other computer. Numbers spreadsheets can be shared online and you just give the link to anyone that needs to view it or edit it.

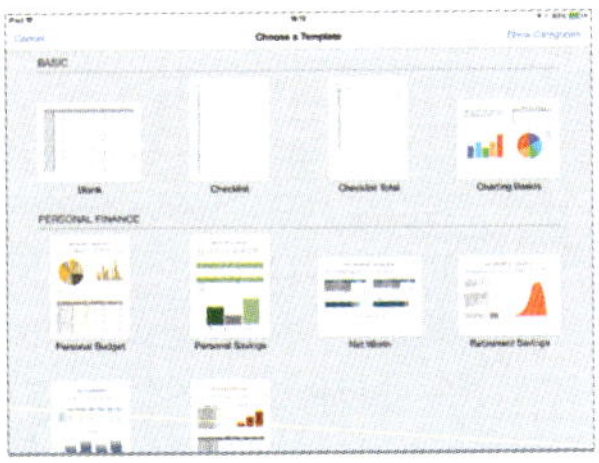

Create a spreadsheet

From the home screen, tap the Create Spreadsheet tile to begin. This displays all the templates and you can choose a blank one and create it from scratch, or select a template that is close to the subject you want.

Using tables

There are two ways to create tables for the data to be entered and you can start with a blank sheet and enter the text and numbers. Afterwards, select everything then go to the format menu and choose a table style. Using the plus button, a table can be inserted into a spreadsheet and it can contain multiple tables, each containing different info. To shrink a table, you can drag up from the bottom-left corner or dragging in from the top-right corner.

Functions and formulas

Like all spreadsheets, Numbers is packed with hundreds of functions and they cover a wide range of topics, such as date and time, duration, engineering, financial, statistical, trigonometric and so on. Functions can tell you the average of a column of numbers, the future value of an investment given the starting amount, the number of years and the interest rate, and they can work out loan repayments. The possibilities are almost endless.

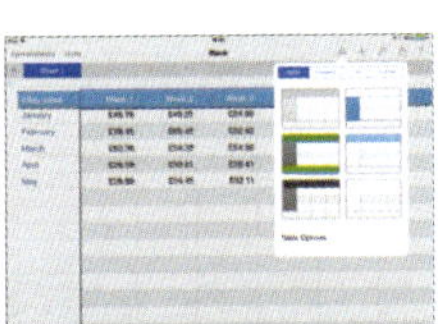

You can use the format menu to change the colours, headers and so on

Create a chart

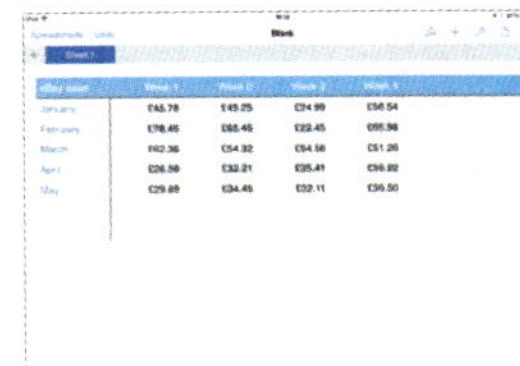

1 The table
Start with a table containing info in several rows and columns.

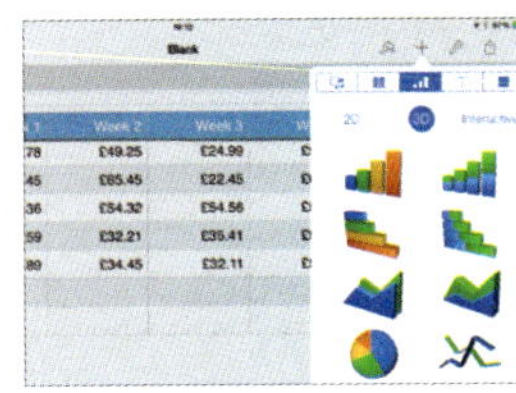

2 Chart types
Press the plus, select 2D, 3D or Interactive, and choose one.

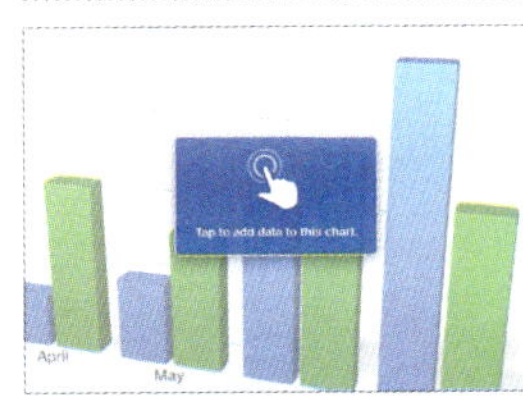

3 Add data
The chart prompts you to tap it to add data and then select cells.

4 Cell selection
Tap and drag the bottom-right corner over the cells to chart.

Keynote

Create slick slideshow presentations on your iPad and share them with others using the Keynote app

You'll use it to...

Create presentations
Use the collection of superb templates

Copy from Pages
Copy and paste information from other apps

Animate objects
Make slides interesting by adding effects and animations

Create notes
Jot down extra notes for use when presenting slideshows

Share presentations
Post slideshows by Mail, Messages and on social networks

Navigate slideshows
Learn secret taps and swipes for navigating your presentations

Create presentations

Keynote creates superb presentations – entertaining slideshows that can contain text, images, music, video clips, charts and animation. A presentation is created by tapping the tile on the home screen, then tap the plus button in the bottom-left corner to add slides.

Features in iOS 9

Keynote has been designed to fit right in with the dynamics of the iOS 9 update. It features iCloud Drive integration, the option to take photos and videos in-app, it features a new custom colour mixer on iPad, has been bolstered with new presenter display layouts, and it also supports third-party storage services and support for Handoff.

Presentations can also be opened, edited and viewed anywhere, making it easier when you are away from your computer and need to show or edit a slideshow on the go. Slideshows are easily shared and there are more ways than in previous versions. AirDrop enables

Fig 1 (above) Combine text and photos, add some animation and you've got an impressive presentation

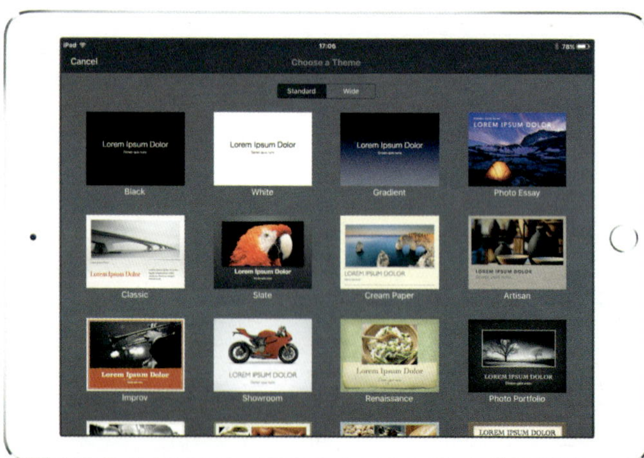

Fig 2 (right) A new interface and exciting new themes make Keynote even better than ever

a presentation to be transferred between devices and computers, and by sharing a link, anyone can access it on the iCloud website. Whatever your slideshow requirement, Keynote is perfect.

Make a slideshow

Create a new presentation and the template opens in the editor. In the top-right corner is a Play button and tapping it plays the slideshow. As you build the presentation, tap the Play button to see the slideshow exactly as your audience will see it.

Navigate your presentation

Thumbnails of each slide in a presentation are shown on the left and tapping a slide opens it for editing or playing. Normally you would press the first slide and the press Play to start the slideshow, but you can jump to any slide and start from there. As a slideshow is playing just tap the screen to advance to the next slide or swipe left to right to step back through. Pinching a running slideshow stops it and you can select a slide to jump to and press Play to restart.

Presenter notes

If you have to talk to an audience while showing them a Keynote presentation, you might want to make notes to help you to remember what to say and when. Each slide can have presenter notes attached that only you can see. Select a slide thumbnail in the left panel of the editor window and press the Tools icon at the top. Select presenter Notes and a notepad and keyboard is displayed for you to create the selected slide's notes. Repeat this for all the slides and use the notes to remind yourself what to say.

Tap on the left to display slide thumbnails and you can then simply tap one to jump to it

Add animations

1 Animate
Tap an object and select Animate. Tap the left build in '+' button.

2 Build in
This animation occurs when the slide opens. Select an effect.

3 Options
The Options tab determines the animation duration and delay.

4 Orderly animations
With two or more animations, set the order by dragging them.